A HOUSE IN ZAMBIA

RECOLLECTIONS OF THE ANC AND OXFAM AT 250 ZAMBEZI ROAD, LUSAKA, 1967-97

edited by

Robin Palmer

Bookworld Publishers

Bookworld Publishers
P.O. Box 32581, Lusaka, Zambia
2008

Preface, Introduction, Chapters 5, 11 and 12 and selection © Robin Palmer 2008
The moral rights of the authors have been asserted

All rights reserved. No part of this publication may be reproduced, stored in a retrieval system, or transmitted, in any form or by any means electronic, mechanical, photocopying, recording or otherwise, without the prior permission of the publisher.

Photographs of Jack and Ray Simons first published in *Comrade Jack* and of 250 Zambezi Rd first published in *All my Life and all my Strength* reproduced by kind permission STE Publishers, South Africa.

ISBN: 978-9982-24-051-2

Printed by
Mission Press

Dedicated to the memory of
Jack Simons (1907-1995),
Ray Alexander Simons (1913-2004),
and
Susanna 'Susie' Smith (1951-2006).

Susie Smith (1951-2006) who began this book and was the inspiration behind its completion.

CONTENTS

Brief Chronology	vii
Note on Contributors	ix
Preface	xiii

I Background — 1
1. *Robin Palmer*, Introduction — 3
2. *Hugh Macmillan*, The Story of a House – 250 Zambezi Road, Roma Township, Lusaka – the Simons, the ANC and Oxfam — 9
3. *Tanya Barben*, 'Entabeni' – A Home in Lusaka away from Home — 29
4. *Peter Wiles*, Oxfam in Southern Africa in the 1980s — 37
5. *Robin Palmer*, Oxfam's Support to the ANC in Zambia in the 1980s — 45

II The Oxfam Representatives in Zambia — 51
6. *Susie Smith* (1979-84) — 53
7. *Anne Lloyd-Williams* (interim, mid 1984) — 65
8. *Mike Edwards* (1984-88) — 67
9. *Pushpanath* (1988-92) — 71
10. *Lucy Muyoyeta* (1993-97) — 75

III The Oxfam Desk Officer and Regional Manager — 81
11. *Robin Palmer* (1987-95) — 83
12. *Robin Palmer* Buying 250 Zambezi Road for Oxfam (1990-92) — 89

IV The Incredible Oxfam Support Staff — 97
13. *Dorothy Chikula* (1980-93) — 99
14. *Malatino Daka* (1980-98) — 109
15. *Wilson Kaonza* (1981-96) — 111
16. *Lazarous Chewe* (1989-95) — 115
17. *Victor Pelekamoyo* (1992-97) — 123

V Some Friends of Oxfam — 129
18. *Gabriel C Banda*, 250 Zambezi Road A Friend's View — 131
19. *Sue Cavanna*, A Recollection of 250 Zambezi Road, Lusaka in 1982-83 — 143

VI Two Postscripts, 2004-05 — 145
20. *Gabriel C Banda*, Susanna 'Susie' Smith returns to Zambia after seventeen years, October 2004 — 147

    21 *Martin Kalungu-Banda*, Susie Smith's final
          visit to Zambia, May 2005   153

7. Closing thoughts   **159**
    22 *Kevin Watkins*, Obituary for Susanna 'Susie' Smith   161
    23 *Izzy Birch (1986-93)*, Closing Thoughts   167

250 ZAMBEZI ROAD – A BRIEF CHRONOLOGY

1965	250 Zambezi Road, Roma, Lusaka ('Entabeni') bought by Jack and Ray Simons
Late 1967	Jack and Ray Simons occupy 250 Zambezi Road
Mid-1979	Oxfam GB moves its Zambia and Malawi office from Blantyre to Lusaka for Front Line States reasons – ANC, SWAPO, UNIN are there
1980	Susanna 'Susie' Smith arrives as Oxfam Field Director for Zambia and Malawi
Late 1980	Susie Smith moves into a house on the 250 Zambezi Road compound, owned by Jack and Ray Simons, leading ANC activists
1984	Mike Edwards succeeds Susie Smith as Oxfam Field Director, later Regional Representative, for Zambia and Malawi
1988	Pushpanath succeeds Mike Edwards as Oxfam Regional Representative for Zambia and Malawi
1990	The Simons decide to return home to South Africa, offer Oxfam first option to buy the whole 250 Zambezi Road compound. Oxfam (Hugh Belshaw) agrees. In a lengthy legal process, Robin Palmer buys it for Oxfam, which then moves its office from Cairo Road into what had been the Simons' house
1992-3	Oxfam Zambia's responses to severest drought for fifty years arguably its finest hour
1993	Lucy Muyoyeta succeeds Pushpanath as Oxfam Regional Representative for Zambia and Malawi
1995	Death of Jack Simons
1995	Oxfam's Malawi programme becomes 'independent' from Zambia
1997	Lucy Muyoyeta steps down as Country Representative for Zambia

2004	Death of Ray Simons
2004	Susie Smith returns to Zambia for the first time since 1987 to work on HIV and AIDS. She starts to write 'a record of the life and times in 250 Zambezi Road' and encourages Mike Edwards and Puspanath to write
2005	Susie Smith's last visit to Zambia, to work on HIV and AIDS. Accompanied by Martin Kalungu-Banda, she meets President Levy Mwanawasa and ex-President Kenneth Kaunda
2006	Death of Susie Smith

NOTE ON CONTRIBUTORS

Robin Palmer taught History at the University of Zambia, 1971-77. He joined Oxfam in 1987, was Desk Officer for Zambia, 1987-91 and Regional Manager for Zambia, 1991-94. He bought 250 Zambezi Road for Oxfam, 1990-92. He later worked on land rights, retired from Oxfam in 2007, and currently works through an Oxford-based consultancy group, Mokoro Ltd.

Hugh Macmillan first visited the Simons at 250 Zambezi Road in January 1969 while doing postgraduate research. He taught History at the University of Zambia, 1978-95 and was a frequent visitor to the Simons and to Susie Smith. He is currently attached to the African Studies Centre at Oxford University and is undertaking research for a book on the history of the ANC in exile in Zambia.

Tanya Barben is the younger daughter of Jack and Ray Simons. She remained in South Africa while her parents were in exile, but made some 20 visits to them in Zambia. She has spent her entire working life in the employ of the University of Cape Town Libraries where she is presently Rare Books Librarian.

Peter Wiles joined Oxfam in 1975, worked in Eastern India until 1980, became Field Secretary for Southern Africa in 1980, the first UK-based Regional Representative for South Africa, Namibia and Lesotho in 1982, and then Area Coordinator for what was called Africa South (East, Central and Southern Africa), 1984-88. After four years as Deputy Director, Child Poverty Action Group in London, he has worked as an international development and humanitarian consultant and is also developing a late career as a photographer.

Susanna 'Susie' Smith was Oxfam's Field Director for Zambia and Malawi, 1980-84, and was the first Oxfam tenant at 250 Zambezi Road from 1980. She worked in Oxford in the Public Affairs Unit, 1985-92, from where she wrote *Front Line Africa – the Right to a Future* (1990) and was a prominent voice in Oxfam's campaigning against apartheid South Africa. She battled against cancer for many years. Her last position in Oxfam was Deputy International Director, 1988-2006. She died on 23 June 2006.

Anne Lloyd-Williams was Oxfam's Desk Officer for Zambia, 1982-87 and acting Field Director for Zambia during part of Susie Smith's maternity leave in mid-1984. She transferred to work on Lusophone Southern and then Francophone Central

A House in Zambia

Africa before leaving Oxfam in 1997. She now works for Windle Trust International on refugee education programmes in Africa.

Michael (Mike) Edwards was Oxfam's Regional Representative for Zambia and Malawi, 1984-88 and lived at 250 Zambezi Road throughout that period. He is now director of the Ford Foundation's Governance and Civil Society Program, based in New York.

Pushpanath Krishnamurthy was Oxfam's Regional Representative for Zambia and Malawi, 1988-92. He later worked for Oxfam in Zimbabwe and the Balkans, and currently works as a Global Campaigner on Climate Change.

Lucy Muyoyeta joined Oxfam Zambia/Malawi in 1985 as Projects Officer. She subsequently became Deputy Regional Representative, then Regional Representative, 1993-95, and Country Representative, 1995-97 after a new office was opened in Malawi. After a short secondment to the West Africa Regional Office, she left Oxfam in 1998 and joined the Open Society in South Africa. She is currently ActionAid's Country Representative in Zambia.

Dorothy Chikula was Oxfam Zambia's first Office Administrator in 1980. She left as Programme Administrator in 1993. Subsequently she worked with Plan International, 1995- 2000, and ActionAid International's Zambian partner HODI, 2001-06, when she retired. She was a friend of Susie Smith for a quarter of a century.

Malitino Daka joined Oxfam Zambia initially as an office clerk in March 1980 and was subsequently promoted to Administrative Assistant/Resources Officer. He established a Resource Centre for Oxfam partners and others which was widely respected and used. He expanded his skills by becoming computer-literate and acquiring a driving licence. He left Oxfam in 1998 and became a self-employed trader, running the 'Fairer World' shop in Lusaka's Mtendere Market.

Wilson Kaonza joined Oxfam Zambia as a driver in March 1980, later becoming Transport Officer responsible for Oxfam's growing fleet of vehicles. He developed an incredible knowledge of the Oxfam's project partners and their history. He retired from Oxfam in 1987 but has continued to drive on occasion for other agencies.

Introduction

Lazarous Chewe joined Oxfam in 1989 as an Administrative Assistant. He acted as guard and night watchman for the 250 Zambezi Road compound. He believes that he gained a great deal from his early exposure to Oxfam and the ANC. He was retrenched in 1995, but went on to acquire a Diploma in Marketing, work for Care International, set up his own business to promote biomass technology, sit on a SADC board on rural energy, study the construction of biomass digesters at the University of Sichuan in China and become a performing musician.

Victor Pelekamoyo worked at 250 Zambezi Road, 1992-97 in various roles as an Accountant on the Oxfam Drought Programme in Eastern Province and later for the Zambia/Malawi Programme. He subsequently worked in Oxfam's Southern African Regional Management Centre in Zimbabwe and is currently a Senior Business Analyst based at Oxfam Headquarters in the UK.

Gabriel C. Banda is an independent development worker and resource person who has been a friend and adviser to Oxfam Zambia since 1980. He has researched and written on a wide range of subjects including debt, drought and Theatre for Development. He has a regular column in *The Post* newspaper and is currently helping former President Kenneth Kaunda to write his memoirs.

Sue Cavanna worked as a VSO in Sichili, Western Province, 1979-83. She started the Sichili Water Wells project with Charles Mwayanguba. Susie Smith gave start-up support with a LandRover, cement for the wells and, through Gabriel Banda, help to develop a Theatre for Development approach. Susie became a very close friend. Sue went on to work in Equatorial Guinea for ACORD, then in Kenya for WaterAid and Maji na Ufanisi, working in the slums of Nairobi and the pastoral drylands. She is now based in Oxford as Director of SOS Sahel UK.

Martin Kalungu-Banda taught Business Ethics at the University of Zambia while also serving as Advocacy Consultant for Oxfam in Zambia, 1996-99. After working for BP Africa as Social Performance Manager, 2000-03, he joined Oxfam in Oxford as head of the Private Sector Policy team. He took a break from Oxfam to serve as Special Consultant to President Mwanawasa of Zambia, 2005-06. In the same period, Susie Smith mentored him on 'Leadership and Innovation to beat the HIV pandemic' work, a precursor to his current position of Global Leadership Adviser in Oxfam's Global Centre of Learning on HIV and AIDS.

A House in Zambia

Kevin Watkins worked for Oxfam as a researcher from 1991-2004, writing widely on trade, debt and poverty issues, including *The Oxfam Poverty Report* (1995) and *Economic Growth with Equity* (1998). He was a regular visitor to 250 Zambezi Road, developed a close working relationship with Oxfam in Zambia and supported Zambian campaigns on debt and other issues. He is currently Director of the UN's Human Development Report Office.

Izzy Birch was Desk Administrator for the Zambia programme based in Oxfam House, Oxford, 1986-93. She then worked for Oxfam GB's Horn and East Africa programme until 2005, developing a specialism in pastoralism. She recently worked for Fahamu, a pan-African human rights organisation, and is now a researcher/ policy adviser to the newly appointed Minister of State for Development of Northern Kenya and Other Arid Lands.

Preface

In October 2004, Susanna (Susie) Smith visited Zambia for the first time in seventeen years to work on HIV and AIDS. She had been Oxfam's Field Director there from 1980-84. She wrote:

> *I was surprised and delighted that quite a few of the Oxfam staff there were interested to know more about the history of our Zambezi Road compound in particular, and Oxfam's history in Zambia in general. So, as promised, this is my personal account of a period in the life of this compound in eastern Lusaka, from 1980 to 1984. It's about the place, the people who made it, and the Oxfam history surrounding it. I am writing it not only for the current staff, but also in memory of the people in this story, so many of whom, it now strikes me, have died. My aim has been to write my bit then pass it on to others connected with the place to add their recollections.*

Susie herself died, on 23 June 2006, after struggling for many years with cancer. After her funeral, a few of us sat down and agreed that it would be a fitting tribute to her and her life to build on the contributions which Susie had gathered from her successors, Mike Edwards and Pushpanath, and from myself as the person who bought 250 Zambezi Road for Oxfam from the South African ANC veterans Jack and Ray Simons.

The Simons had rented a house on the compound to Susie and her successors, and for a decade there were strong links between 250 Zambezi Road, the Simons, the ANC, and Oxfam Zambia.

This collection is an attempt to capture some of that time through the recollections of some of people who lived and worked there during the 1980s and 1990s. They were remarkable times and remarkable people and I hope that some of what made them special is reflected here.

PART ONE:

BACKGROUND

1. A HOUSE IN ZAMBIA – INTRODUCTION

Robin Palmer

This is a story about a house with a history, about some of the remarkable people who lived or worked there, and about its place in the liberation struggle for Southern Africa. It also tries to capture something of the spirit of the times in the worlds of politics and development, and it focuses on the links which were established between Oxfam GB in Zambia and the African National Congress (ANC) of South Africa.[1]

Though the origins of this work were tinged with sadness, as stated in the preface, the process of writing it has been a hugely enjoyable and rewarding one. The contributors have sought to inform and stimulate each other as successive contributions have been received, and even to suggest new avenues – as for example the story of Oxfam's support to the ANC in Zambia in chapter 5.

Zambia as a Frontline State

I had the great privilege of living and working in Zambia during the 1970s. Zambia was then a key Frontline State in the struggle between white settler-controlled Southern Africa (South Africa, South-West Africa, Rhodesia, Portuguese West and East Africa) and countries to the north, such as Zambia, Botswana and Tanzania, which had achieved independence under majority rule in the 1960s. The struggle was long, bloody and bitter. An army coup in Portugal in 1974, brought about by long, unwinnable colonial wars, resulted in independence for Mozambique and Angola in 1975 – and the restoration of democracy itself in Portugal after a fascist dictatorship lasting fifty years. The advent of the new FRELIMO government in Mozambique increased the pressures on Ian Smith's rebel Rhodesia (Zambia's neighbour), which finally lost its unwinnable war. The country became independent as Zimbabwe in 1980. It took a further decade of struggle before South-West Africa became independent Namibia in 1990.

---

[1] A Mokoro colleague Mary Betley reminded me of another history of a house with ANC connections, in Swaziland. Elias Masilela, *Number 43 Trelawney Park – KwaMagogo*, David Philip, Cape Town, 2006. For details, see:
http://www.newafricabooks.co.za/books_detail.asp?ID=674

Finally, in South Africa, the ANC was unbanned in 1990, a new constitution was written, and the country's first democratic elections were held in 1994, when Nelson Mandela became South Africa's first black president.

The 1970s and 1980s were difficult decades for Zambia, as the country was forced to pay *The High Price of Principles*, to cite the title of Richard Hall's 1970 book about *Kaunda and the White South*. Zambia housed freedom fighters from the 'white south' and so suffered air attacks and numerous other incursions. Zambia closed its border with neighbouring Rhodesia, attempting to apply the sanctions which Britain had called for but so lamentably failed to implement. Britain's pusillanimous handling of Rhodesia's UDI was both a scandal and a cause of much misery and frustration to land-locked Zambia. The building of the Tazara railway from Zambia to the port of Dar es Salaam was an attempt to address this. The country suffered repeated shortages of basic commodities and President Kaunda was frequently criticised for paying too much attention to foreign affairs.

But the important thing to capture is that Zambia was a free country, a decent, tolerant place, even within a one-party system, where people didn't kill each other because of politics. It was also an island of peace and sanity in contrast to its war-stricken neighbours or the rotten dictatorship which was Malawi under Kamuzu Banda. Many of the students I taught at the University of Zambia (UNZA) in the 1970s came from other countries in Southern Africa. They were overwhelmingly glad to be living and studying in Zambia.

Jack and Ray Simons

In 1965 two distinguished South African exiles arrived in Zambia. They were Jack and Ray Simons, and they feature prominently in this book. They bought what Zambians call a 'compound', a piece of land on which they subsequently built three houses. This was 250 Zambezi Road ('Entabeni'), in the suburb of Roma in Lusaka, the capital city of Zambia. They took occupancy of this compound in 1967, and they lived there until 1990 when, greatly to their surprise, they were able to return home to South Africa. Neither had expected to live long enough for this to happen; Jack died in 1995, aged 88; Ray in 2004, aged 90. The rapid pace of change in South Africa, accelerated by the fall of Communism (which meant that the apartheid regime could no longer play the anti-communist card which had been so successful during the Reagan – Thatcher years), took all of us so-called 'experts' by surprise.

Introduction

In chapter 2, Hugh Macmillan writes engagingly about the Simons and their time in exile in Zambia, and how 250 Zambezi Road became a centre of ANC activities. He is currently writing a history of the ANC in exile in Zambia. In chapter 3, Tanya Barben, daughter of the Simons, talks about her visits to her parents at 250 Zambezi Road. In 1980, the 28 year old Susanna Smith (as she was then known) arrived in Lusaka as the Oxfam GB 'Field Director' for Zambia and Malawi. As both Susie and Peter Wiles write here (in chapters 6 and 4), Oxfam had just moved its office from Malawi to Zambia in order to better attune itself to the realities of the Frontline States and the struggle against apartheid South Africa and Namibia. The facts that the ANC and SWAPO (the South West Africa People's Organisation) were present in Zambia, as was the United Nations Institute for Namibia (UNIN), were important considerations. Later Susie Smith (as she called herself in Oxford) was to play a pivotal role in challenging the constraints of British charity law when Oxfam ran its 1990 Frontline Africa campaign, arguing that apartheid was a direct cause of poverty in South Africa and that Britain should therefore apply economic sanctions.

Oxfam as tenants of the Simons

In late 1980, Susanna Smith became a tenant of Jack and Ray Simons at 250 Zambezi Road. Thus began a decade of close, almost intimate, connection, as she was succeeded in turn by Mike Edwards (in 1984) and Pushpanath (in 1988). All three write about their experiences in this collection. In her wonderfully evocative piece, Susie writes:

> all I can attempt is to write about them as the remarkable people I had the good fortune to live near, their friendship, and their huge impact on me as a young person trying to understand Southern Africa.

Jack and Ray were charismatic figures, in their different ways, hugely experienced and generous with their knowledge. They also provided valuable introductions to the various ANC figures who passed through Lusaka. In chapter 5 we tell the previously untold story of how Oxfam funded, in a very small way, some ANC activities in Zambia during the 1980s. As Mike Edwards recalls, 'solidarity funding – those were the days!'

In 1990, the Simons were able to return home and they offered Oxfam first option on the purchase of 250 Zambezi Road. I was Oxfam's Desk

Officer for Zambia at the time, and in chapter 12 I tell the complex story of how I came to buy the compound for Oxfam. It was a long drawn out, tortuous affair, in which Hugh Macmillan, as a friend of both sides, played an heroic intermediary role. Oxfam then moved its office from downtown Lusaka to Zambezi Road, in the leafy suburb of Roma. As Pushpanath's successor (in 1993) Lucy Muyoyeta notes, 'we did not know it then, but we were amongst the pioneers of the decamping of offices from the city into the suburbs.'

An Oxfam oasis

So Oxfam came to take possession of 250 Zambezi Road and is still there, almost twenty years later. As many of our contributors testify, there was created during the early 1990s a quite remarkable, very tangible atmosphere about the place, which I believe owed something to its previous owners. The critical point was that the Oxfam office was open and accessible to all at all times – including partners from any part of the country, development workers such as Gabriel Banda, and students and academics wishing to use the valuable Resources Centre built up by the remarkable Malitino Daka. 'Through those doors many, many people came', writes Lucy Muyoyeta. Gabriel Banda recalled that '250 Zambezi Road was then an oasis, a place for nourishment and inspiration.' As the dynamic, young accountant, Victor Pelekamoyo recalls in chapter 17:

> *As an outsider, I wondered why Oxfam laboured so much to make the partners feel that Oxfam existed because of them and not the other way round...Oxfam Zambia believed in its partners and its partners believed in it. Most importantly, partners felt welcome and wanted whenever they visited 250 Zambezi Road.*

The marvellous chapter by Victor illustrates a feature that I am particularly proud of in this collection – the quite astonishing ways in which what I've called Oxfam's incredible support staff have responded to the opportunity to carry on the story which Susie began, of remarkable people and remarkable times, as seen through their own eyes, in chapters 13-17. In doing so, they have enriched this work immeasurably.

Some failures

Not all was sweetness and light at 250 Zambezi Road, of course, and nor was the place without its conflicts. At the same time I joined Oxfam in 1987, Oxfam also created the new post of Regional Development Officer for Southern Africa. The person appointed was Caroline Allison (now Roseveare). I was also her Desk Officer and she was based in Lusaka. She had a nightmare of a time, as did her successor, the Tanzanian, Loserian Sangale. The post, though created by Oxfam Southern Africa collectively, proved to be an endless source of conflict, both under Mike Edwards and then Pushpanath. On reflection, this was because Oxfam was clearly not ready for a regional post of this kind. Now the whole organization is regionalized, but back then it was run on strictly national lines, with the Field Directors, later Country (or Regional) Representatives accustomed to brooking no interference within 'their' territory. We just didn't think it through properly and so much of the unproductive heat generated was personalized, when really we should have been looking at structures, roles and responsibilities.

A second failure was the difficulty of handling those occasions when it was deemed necessary to make staff redundant. This comes through in several contributions, and in chapter 13 Dorothy Chikula recalls vividly the pain of her departure from Oxfam, but also how she subsequently found the strength to recover from that shock and to regard it as a blessing in disguise.

AIDS

This collection focuses on the 1980s and 1990s, but it concludes, fittingly I believe, with the stories of Susie Smith's last two visits to Zambia, after seventeen years' absence, in October 2004 and May 2005. Susie, then coming towards the end of a long and courageous battle against cancer, was much exercised by the scourge of AIDS which has decimated Zambia. She met with former President, Kenneth Kaunda, and current President, Levi Mwanawasa, to express her concerns. As Martin Kalungu-Banda writes, a cross-sector trust has been set up to respond to this scourge; 'Susie is regarded by the Trust as the spirit that inspired its work. In Zambia, Susie lives.'

Final words

We produce here a slightly revised version of the obituary for Susie written for *The Guardian* by Kevin Watkins, formerly a leading Oxfam policy analyst, who had close personal and professional links with both Susie and Oxfam Zambia. But fittingly, the final words and closing thoughts come from my long-time friend and collaborator, Izzy Birch. She and I worked on the Zambia Desk in Oxford for six years. It was a fruitful relationship, in which we tried to give all the support we could to the remarkable women and men we called 'the Zammers' – the staff and partners from Zambia whose work we so much admired. Izzy did battle on their behalf on numerous occasions, not least over contentious issues of salaries, union representation and, when it came to it, redundancy packages. Dorothy Chikula remembers her as 'our guardian angel who did so much for us in Zambia, made a lot of difference in our working lives, and was a very key person in the life of Oxfam Zambia, during our time.'

Izzy reminds us that so many who feature in this collection have now died. May they rest in peace, and may *A House in Zambia* pay a proper tribute to some of their extraordinary achievements.

250 Zambezi Road, c.1970

2. THE STORY OF A HOUSE – 250 ZAMBEZI ROAD, ROMA TOWNSHIP, LUSAKA – THE SIMONS, THE ANC AND OXFAM

Hugh Macmillan

My links with the Simons and 250 Zambezi Road

My association with 250 Zambezi Road goes back nearly forty years. I have some knowledge of the four main dimensions of its remarkable history – as the home of Jack and Ray Simons, as a significant place in the history of the African National Congress and of the liberation struggle in Southern Africa, as the home of Susanna Smith and successive country representatives of Oxfam, and as the Oxfam office and a developmental centre. Speaking as a historian, I can say without much fear of contradiction that there can be few houses, or housing complexes, in Lusaka that have welcomed so many interesting people or witnessed so much history in the making.

I first crossed the threshold of the main house in January 1969 when it was not much more than a year old and the garden was undeveloped. I was doing historical research in Zambia and had come to see Jack and Ray Simons who were old friends of my parents – my father had known Jack before he left South Africa in 1932 and they had mutual respect for each other as academics and intellectuals. My first visit was at the height of the rainy season and Zambezi Road was muddy and not yet tarred, nor were many of the neighbouring houses built. In 1969 only the nucleus of the Simons' house was there – the long back veranda which was the usual entrance, the enclosed veranda which is now the front entrance. Jack's study and the archive room, to the right of that entrance, were added at later dates. The cottage was built circa 1968 to provide accommodation for Oliver Tambo, Acting President of the ANC, who was primarily based in Lusaka from 1967 onwards. The military headquarters moved there from Morogoro in preparation for the launch in August of that year of the Wankie campaign, an invasion of Southern Rhodesia in alliance with the Zimbabwe African People's Union (ZAPU). Lusaka became the de facto headquarters of the ANC in 1967, though it did not formally move its headquarters from Morogoro until the early 1980s.

Tambo did not stay for long in the cottage, but it was later occupied by a succession of ANC people including Archie Sibeko (Zola Zembe), trade unionist and Umkhonto weSizwe (MK) logistics operative, Ruth Mompati, and the Masondos. Andrew Masondo, a former Maths lecturer at the University of Fort Hare and Robben Island prisoner, became the political commissar of MK, and, after liberation, a general in the South African Defence Force. Cecilia, his wife, was Oliver Tambo's private secretary for many years - she died in Lusaka in 1990 as she was preparing to return to South Africa after many years in exile. The house that Susie occupied in 1980, which became the Oxfam representative's house, had been built and lived in by the Simons' son, Johan, a few years previously – its first tenant was Juan Fernandez, a Cuban diplomat.

Jack Simons

Jack and Ray Simons (she was well known in South Africa as Ray Alexander, in exile as Ray Simons, and in South Africa, latterly, as Ray Alexander Simons) had been forced to leave South Africa in May 1965. Jack was born at Riversdale in the then Cape Colony on 7 February 1907 and joined the South African civil service after leaving school. He did a first degree by correspondence, and, after completing an MA in South Africa, proceeded in 1932 to the London School of Economics where he finished a doctoral dissertation in 1936. He became politically active in London and joined the Communist Party there – he saw it as providing the strongest opposition to the rise of fascism. He returned to South Africa in 1937 and joined the staff of the University of Cape Town where he worked as a lecturer, and later professor, of African Law and Government for nearly thirty years. He was widely regarded as the most inspiring teacher on the staff. He became a member of the central committee of the then apparently moribund Communist Party of South Africa in the late1930s and, with Ray and Moses Kotane, played a major role in the revival of the party. He was detained and charged in connection with the African mineworkers strike in 1946 and was, with Ray, listed as a communist when the party was banned in terms of the Suppression of Communism Act in 1950.

Ray Simons

Ray was born at Varkalan in the province of Kurland in the then Russian Empire on 31 December 1913 (Old Style – 12 January by the modern calendar, though she always celebrated her birthday on the last day of the year). She became involved in radical politics in what had become the independent state of Latvia and emigrated to South Africa in 1929. She joined the Communist Party of South Africa (CPSA) within a week of arriving in Cape Town and began to play a part in the organisation of trade unions while still a teenager – she became a member of the CPSA central committee at the age of twenty-three. She was involved with many non-racial trade unions, but is best remembered as the founder of the Food and Canning Workers Union in 1941. She was banned from trade union work in 1953 and was then elected to the South African Parliament to represent African voters in the Western Cape, but the law was changed to prevent her from taking her seat. She was also a founder of the non-racial Federation of South African Women. She continued to be involved in underground trade union work after her banning, and also did much of the research for the book *Class and Colour in South Africa, 1850-1950*, which she and Jack published in 1969.

The Simons settle in Lusaka

When Jack was banned from teaching in 1964 they had no means of earning a living and had to leave South Africa, which they did in May 1965, travelling by car with a friend through Southern Rhodesia. They left their three children, Mary, Tanya and Johan, at university and school in Cape Town, and, wishing to settle as near as they could to South Africa, they chose newly independent Zambia. Jack's colleague, the social anthropologist, Monica Wilson, had written to President Kaunda on their behalf, and they carried a letter with them from Chief Albert Luthuli, then President of the banned ANC, saying that he was sending them to him in Zambia 'on loan'. They were initially given a permit to stay for ten days and it was not until August 1965 that they got permission to stay longer. There was then suspicion in both Zambia and Tanzania of white South African communists and it took lobbying by old friends, Nephas Tembo and Simon Zukas, and the intervention of Simon Kapwepwe, to secure their residence permits which were eventually signed by Kaunda. Jack investigated the possibility of getting a job at the University of Zambia and was told that it would help if he had his own accommodation. Jack and Ray bought the Zambezi Road plot and gave instructions for the building of the house during what was intended to be a year's absence – it turned out to be two years' absence - in Manchester where Jack had a visiting fellowship at the university. Ray returned on a visit in July 1966 and was distressed by the slow progress of the building and the inadequate size of the rooms in the house, but she soon sorted that out.

Jack and Ray did not return to live in their new house until 7 December 1967. Although it was never used and not often noticed, the house had a name and there was a name plate on the wall – 'Entabeni' – both the name and the plate came from their house in Oranjezicht, Cape Town, which was placed on the slopes of Table Mountain and had a magnificent view of the city. The name had been given to the original house by an African clergyman and carried a double meaning in isiXhosa, referring both to its location under the mountain and its role as a place of refuge. Jack started work as a Professor of Sociology at UNZA in the following year while Ray began work as an administrative assistant at the ILO. Oliver Tambo invited them to join the ANC in January 1968 – this was more than a year before the official opening of the ANC to non-African exiles by a decision of the Morogoro Conference. Tambo then said that he hoped that they would work to revive the ANC underground in South Africa and with the international anti-apartheid movement.

Crisis in the ANC

Jack and Ray soon became involved in a crisis that gripped the ANC in Lusaka in the aftermath of the failure of the Wankie and Sipolilo campaigns in Southern Rhodesia. Chris Hani, later Chief of Staff of MK, and General Secretary of the (underground) South African Communist Party (SACP), was a commander of what was called the Luthuli Detachment in the Wankie campaign. He had been imprisoned with other members of the detachment for a year or more in Botswana and, on their release in the later months of 1968, he and six other members of the 'Cape group' wrote a memorandum which was highly critical of the leadership. The majority of the members of a military tribunal voted for their execution and, according to Hani himself, they were only saved from this fate by the determined intervention of Mzwai Piliso, later head of the security department.[1] According to another account 'dungeons' were dug for their incarceration on a farm near Livingstone, but they were saved from that fate by Oliver Tambo, who took

---

1 See Vladimir Shubin, *ANC: A View from Moscow*, Belville, Mayibuye Books, 1999, 88-93 for an account of the 'Hani Memorandum' and its consequences.

personal responsibility for the failings of the ANC and suggested that the legitimate complaints of the seven had been exploited by members of the leadership. They were tried by a second tribunal and suspended from the ANC in March 1969, but were granted an amnesty and reinstated after the Morogoro Conference in May 1969.[2] According to both Ray Simons and Livingstone Mqotsi, an 'expelled' member of the Unity Movement and secondary school teacher with whom Hani was sent to stay after his release from Botswana, there was a plot to kill Hani, possibly involving people who felt frustrated by this reprieve, though the sequence of events is not entirely clear. Hani told Mqotsi that he had saved his life when he refused entry to the house to a group of MK 'boys' who came looking for him at midnight. Ray was informed of this by 'Comrade [Dingo] Hashe' and sought to contact Oliver Tambo who was out of town. She summoned Thomas Nkobi, the ANC's chief representative in Zambia, to see her at the ILO office where she was working and warned him that Hani's death would have disastrous consequences for the international reputation of the ANC. There were apparently subsequent meetings at 250 Zambezi Road that defused the tension. Hani acknowledged the support that Jack had given him and the other signatories during their period of suspension and 'isolation'. Some members of the ANC in Lusaka were unhappy at the reinstatement of the seven, and at Hani's subsequent promotion, and there was a mutiny which rumbled on into 1971. The ANC sought to expel thirty of its defiant members late in 1970 – they had refused an order to move out of Lusaka to a 'bush' camp – but the Zambian Government was not very happy with this move. It wanted the ANC to control its members, not to expel them.[3]

Arms and arrests

There was another drama in August 1970 when the house was raided by the police and two prominent members of the ANC, MK Chief of Staff, Mxwaku Mjojo (now General Lennox Lagu), and Zola (Wilson) Nqose, who had been transporting arms and ammunition from MK's eastern front

---

2 Evidence in ANC archives at Fort Hare University and from interviews with Alfred Sipetho Willie and Major-General Gardner Sijake, Cape Town, 5 April 2008.
3 Notes of interviews with Ray Simons and Livingstone Mqotsi and evidence from ANC archives.

to its western front - probably from Feira, now Luangwa, to Livingstone - were found sleeping in the cottage with two packing cases containing sixty-eight AK47s and ammunition. They were arrested and later sentenced to prison terms. A week or so later Jack was detained and held at Kabwe high security prison for several days. Archie Sibeko and Ray Simons gave rather different accounts of these events.[4]

There's no dispute that Archie Sibeko had given the key to the cottage to his comrades and that they were, unknown to Jack and Ray, using 250 Zambezi Road for the storage of arms and ammunition. The main dispute is about the reason for the police entering the compound. According to Sibeko, Ray was in dispute with a neighbour who had dumped a load of smelly manure near her fence. She had reported them to the council and, in retaliation, they had complained to the police about foreign-registered Land Rovers 'driving in and out at all times of the day and night'. According to Ray, on the other hand, the police had come to investigate a murder that had taken place in the next street – the comrades had not locked the gate and the murderers had run into the yard. The police raided the cottage and the house. They didn't find the murderers, but they did find the sleeping comrades with their arms cache. The next day, Sunday, the police came again and told Jack and Ray not to move anything. Jack summoned Archie Sibeko's friend, Joyce Leeson, who was doing socio-medical research at the university, and told her what had happened. He also told her not to move anything, but she and Archie buried material under boards in the garden. The police came again the following day and made a further search. Ray recalled that she was standing on a board under which weapons were concealed – she didn't indicate whether she knew they were there or not.

It was on the following Saturday that Jack was detained – he had been warned the previous day by a Zambian woman that he was about to be arrested. A great deal of lobbying by Oliver Tambo, Zambian political allies including Justin Chimba and Nephas Tembo, was required to secure Jack's release. Fitzpatrick Chuula also helped as did one of Jack's students who

---

4 Archie Sibeko (Zola Zembe), *Freedom in Our Lifetime*, Durban: Indicator Press, University of Natal, 1996, 95-6; notes of conversations with Ray Simons. The implication of Sibeko's published account is that these events took place in August 1968, but there is no doubt that they actually took place in August 1970.

was with the Office of the President. Ray was certain that Aaron Milner, Kaunda's security supremo, was determined to deport them. She said that this was not ruled out until the matter was discussed at a cabinet meeting in February 1971. She also said that when Kaunda was asked about his signature of a detention order for Jack, he said that he had believed that he was signing an order for an Anglo-American Corporation employee called Sayman. This incident occurred at a very sensitive time when, in preparation for the Non-Aligned Conference at the newly built Mulungushi Hall, all liberation movements had been asked to remove their cadres from Lusaka. Oliver Tambo set up an internal commission into the 'incidents in Roma township' under the chairmanship of Alfred Nzo.[5]

It was in the same month – August 1970 – that a leading member of the ANC's National Executive Committee, Flag Boshielo (also known as Mkgomane) set off from 250 Zambezi Road with three others in a desperate attempt to get 'home' to South Africa. It is believed that they were betrayed and that three of them were killed while crossing the Caprivi Strip. The fourth member of the group was taken prisoner but was never heard of again. Ray recalled that Flag and his comrades were doctoring themselves with herbs from the garden at a time when she was preparing to leave for an ILO conference in Bulgaria. She begged them not to leave, but found on her return that, tragically, they had already done so.

Walking the neighbourhood

Life for Jack and Ray was not all drama. They had soon established a regular daily rhythm. They got up early and regularly worked sixteen-hour days, but there was always a break in the late afternoon for a walk around Roma, which often took them through N'gombe compound where Jack, especially, was a well-known personality, stopping to chat to many acquaintances among Roma's domestic working population. Writing to his old friend, Julius Lewin, who was trying to persuade him to retire to the UK, as he and his wife had done, Jack provided a pastoral picture of their life as it was in 1972, emphasising the economy of their quasi-peasant existence in what was still an almost rural environment.

---

5   Notes of conversations with Ray Simons and documents in ANC archives.

> *I wear, for work, an open-neck shirt and a washable pair of khaki trousers, with sandals or a cheap veldskoen type of shoe; our two-acre plot supplies all the fruit and vegetables we need, including jams and marmalades; I live within walking distance of the university, and three miles from the shopping and business centre; and run a car which with licence and insurance costs about £15 a month. Rates, water and electricity amount to another £15 a month; and our gardener is paid £20 (high by local standards). We have access to two good libraries, watch TV when so inclined, and decline more invitations to parties than we accept....not being city-bred, I prefer the open spaces, and am at home in this combination of urbanism and rural environment. Five minutes walking from the house brings us into the bush – a mixture of tall grasses and shrubs or clusters of trees – away from roads and motor vehicles. We could not so easily escape the roar of the city in England.*[6]

Jack and Ray were not only involved with the ANC, SWAPO, ZAPU, MPLA and FRELIMO, all of whose leaders visited 250 Zambezi Road, but also made a contribution to the political life of Zambia. This was through links with the trade unions and was most conspicuous in the later 1970s when Jack worked tirelessly to promote 'scientific socialism' within the ruling United National Independence Party (UNIP). The temporary move to the left had been prompted by events in Angola and the strong opposition which had been expressed by students and others to the government's closeness to UNITA and its initial reluctance to recognise the MPLA government. It was also in the late 1970s that Jack, who was already in his seventies, spent long periods in the ANC's camps in Angola. He played an important role in the political education of the recruits who left South Africa after the Soweto Uprising in 1976. Many of them came to the ANC from the Black Consciousness Movement and had little knowledge of the history of the liberation struggle, or of Marxism, and some of them were sceptical about non-racialism. Jack's skills as a teacher – he was an exponent of the Socratic method – were greatly appreciated by the youth, as were his immense knowledge of South African history and politics, his sense of humour, and his passionate commitment to socialism and non-racialism.

---

6   Jack Simons to Julius Lewin, 7 March 1972, Lewin Papers, Cullen Library, University of the Witwatersrand, Johannesburg.

The Story of a House

A violent incident

I became a regular visitor to 250 Zambezi Road at the beginning of 1978 when I came from Swaziland to work at UNZA. Jack was then away for a few months - he was giving political education courses in the ANC's military camps in Angola. It was in June of the following year that Jack was the victim of a violent incident at the gate. He and Ray were returning from their regular afternoon walk when they were mugged and Jack was shot in the foot. A pistol bullet passed between two of his toes. The injury could have been much more serious, but it was painful and a nasty shock for both of them. I was visiting Swedish friends in Kazungula Road and heard the shot, but I didn't know what had happened until a bit later on. The Cuban diplomat, Juan Fernandez, was first on the scene and provided first aid. My girlfriend, and later wife, Monica Ndovi, who was then a midwife at the University Teaching Hospital, played her part in Jack's recovery by supplying a rare and powerful antiseptic known as EUSO – an acronym for Edinburgh University solution – which seemed to have a magical effect. Jack never ceased to remind Ray that in this moment of crisis she had called upon God for help – she had, of course, been brought up as an Orthodox Jew – and he wanted to know why, as a good communist, she had not called upon Marx or Lenin!

This incident was particularly alarming because Jack and Ray were, like other prominent members of the ANC and the SACP, possible targets for assassination. The South African spy, Craig Williamson, who later admitted responsibility for the murder of Ruth First, had visited 250 Zambezi Road earlier in the year, claiming that he had been sent by Mary Simons. He was then working for the Inter-University Exchange Fund, but Ray was deeply suspicious of him and warned her comrades against him. In spite of very real security risks Jack and Ray kept an open house at 250 Zambezi Road for members of the ANC and other liberation movements. There can have been very few members of the ANC in Lusaka – a population which grew from a few hundred in the late 1960s to three or four thousand in the late 1980s – who did not visit the house at one time or another.

Some visitors

Among those who stayed as a guest in the main house for long periods in the 1980s was Moses Mabhida who became General Secretary of the

SACP in 1981 and died in Maputo in 1986. He was a man of few words, at least when I was around, and I remember how he would always withdraw to his room immediately after supper in much the same way that monks retire to their cells. There was also, of course, Sam Nkwe (or Poho) whom Susie remembered. Jack had recruited him from the Angolan camps to the political education department. He had been asthmatic in his youth and Sam's asthma created a bond between them. Almost daily visitors at times in the 1980s included Joe Slovo, Chris Hani, John Nkadimeng and Reg September. Oliver Tambo, Thabo Mbeki, Mac Maharaj, Ronnie Kasrils, and other prominent leaders of the ANC, were, as far as I could tell, less frequent visitors, though I was almost always an afternoon visitor and a bit vague about who came in the mornings. I recall that Tambo visited on Jack's eightieth birthday in 1987. After his release from Robben Island, Herman Toivo ja Toivo, the SWAPO leader, and an old friend from Cape Town, was an occasional visitor. Latterly, Jack and Ray, who were unfailingly hospitable to all visitors, were somewhat overwhelmed by the huge entourage with which he, as Vice-President of SWAPO, and the soon-to-be Vice-President of Namibia, arrived at Zambezi Road.

From the mid 1980s there was also an increasing flow of visitors from inside South Africa. The Simons' daughters, Mary and Tanya (see chapter 3), had been regular visitors from Cape Town from Christmas 1967 onwards, but in 1976 they were banned and placed under house arrest. They were not able to visit Lusaka again until after their banning orders were lifted five years later. Among the early visitors from South Africa whom I remember meeting at 250 Zambezi Road was Professor H. W. van der Merwe, an Afrikaner and Quaker peacemaker, who came for the first time in 1981. He came back again several times in 1984-5. I met him again in December 1984 when he came with Piet Muller, an editor of the Afrikaans newspaper, Beeld. Both van der Merwe and Muller came to Lusaka in 1984 with the knowledge of elements in the South African government, and its security apparatus, and reported back to them. Their visits were early feelers in the path towards negotiations, on which, at the Kabwe Conference in the following year, the ANC leadership was given permission in principle to embark.

It was also in 1984 that I took David Webster, a social anthropologist and a leading member of the newly formed United Democratic Federation (UDF) to meet Jack and Ray. Unknown in advance to me or to David,

Thabo Mbeki was waiting there to meet him and, during a conversation, gave him a secret number or address which, I remember, he carefully copied on to a banknote as I drove him to the airport. Tragically, David was assassinated outside his house in Johannesburg in May 1989 – less than a year before the un-banning of the ANC. His assassin, Ferdi Barnard, who did not apply for amnesty for this murder, is now serving a life sentence. After the meeting in September 1985 at Mfuwe between leaders of the ANC and the Anglo American group of businessmen, there was a continuous stream of visitors from South Africa to the ANC in Lusaka and many of them made their way to 250 Zambezi Road.

My links with Oxfam

My association with Susie and Oxfam in Zambia must have begun soon after her arrival in the country and probably before she reached 250 Zambezi Road, but we got to know each other well after she moved in. I'm not quite sure whether Bobby, her famous dog, came with her or arrived later, but I know that he remained a formidable presence at the gate for many years during her stay and after her departure. As she recalled (chapter 6) we often accompanied Jack and Ray on their daily walks around Roma and N'gombe compound. In a message that she sent to me not long before her death, she recalled that we were privileged to walk with 'the cleverest man in the world'! Jack certainly was an exceptional man – he was a polymath and was interested in everything and everybody. He was also one of those unusual people who have the ability to raise the level of a conversation into the intellectual stratosphere and to ask apparently simple, but really fundamental, questions. I've always thought that my weekly walks and talks with Jack over twelve years were an important part of my education. When Susie's mother, Prudence Smith, came on a visit I found that I had a link with her too. She was a South African who had worked for the BBC and produced programmes on African topics. She had produced at least one talk by Jack and had also produced talks by my own father – I was pleased to hear her say what a good broadcaster he had been.

Through Susie I also got to know the remarkable group of fellow workers she recruited for the Oxfam office, then in Cairo Road. They included Dorothy Chikula, Francis Banda and the man I always thought of as 'Mr Daka'. I'm very grateful to Susie for the opportunity that she later gave me to do a bit of work for Oxfam. When she was expecting Sarah, she was unable to undertake long journeys and in January 1983 she asked me to go on her behalf to check out the position of the refugees and local people in Senanga West. The area had suffered from a series of South African invasions between 1979 and 1982. It was a great privilege for an UNZA lecturer to be able to travel to one of the most remote corners of the country in Oxfam's Toyota Land Cruiser and to be driven there by Wilson Kaonza – a man of great charisma and a driver with the most remarkable knowledge of the languages, highways and byways of Zambia, though even he took a wrong turning in the trackless plains of Senanga West. He was to become a great friend – so much so that I passed on to him two remarkable old crocks – the much-loved (by me, though not by my wife and son) VW Beetle that I had driven up from Swaziland via Botswana and Kazungula in 1978, and driven around Lusaka for twelve years until 1990, and the equally historical Renault which I had taken over from Jack when he and Ray left the country in that year.

    I'm not sure that the report that I wrote for Oxfam was of any great value to it, but the journey was significant for me. It was on this journey which took me to the Angolan border at Kaunga Mashi – I only discovered much later that the place was only a stone's throw away from Jonas Savimbi's and UNITA's then active headquarters at Jamba – that I first learnt about the post-independence underdevelopment of the Western Province. It was then that I first heard of the sad demise of Susman Brothers & Wulfsohn's chain of rural stores which had once bought cattle and other produce, and supplied goods in these remote places. I didn't know then that twenty years later I would write a large book on the history of the business.[7] Susie had a great interest in the people of Sichili where Oxfam had projects and it was only when writing this book that I realised that Sichili was very close to Mulobezi, the centre of timber milling for Zambesi Saw Mills, which was also part of the story. During our last email correspondence Susie sent me some photographs she had taken of dilapidated locomotives at Mulobezi.

    Among my most vivid memories of that journey are of Wilson wrestling with a fire of grass seeds under the vehicle, and using the winch attached to

---

[7] Hugh Macmillan. *An African Trading Empire: The Story of Susman Brothers & Wulfsohn, 1901–2005*. New York: I. B.Tauris, 2005.

a tree to pull us out of one tricky spot. I also remember eating hippo meat – poached in Angola by a Mr Lance – at Sipupa. I think it was there that I met an old teacher who could have given seminars on aid and underdevelopment. I remember him looking at a beautiful new Norad well and asking if Norad would come back to fix it when it stopped working. For some reason Oxfam was distributing cassava sticks to the local inhabitants and I remember the old teacher looking at them and saying that colonial officials had distributed the same type thirty years previously. His last word on the subject was: 'You know they don't grow here, but if you insist we will plant them...' One thing that I learnt very quickly was that if you asked people if they were short of food they would always say 'yes', so I stopped asking.

I remember telling Susie's successor, Mike Edwards, that I had really not been prepared to peep into people's grain bins to assess their food supplies. He seemed to think that this indicated a distinct lack of rigour on my part, but then Mike in those days was a serious, not to say earnest, young man. Even Jack and Ray, who were rarely idle, tended to think that he was a bit of a workaholic. Not long before he left for a sabbatical at an Indian ashram in 1988, it was good to meet his South American girlfriend and future wife, Cora Anne Castro, on a visit to Zambia. I've been impressed to learn recently that Mike was developing during his time at 250 Zambezi Road a major critique of development studies and that he has moved to Washington and become a Ford Foundation guru. I was equally impressed to learn of Susie's important contribution to the development of Oxfam's role in advocacy and to bringing about changes in charity law in the United Kingdom.

The Simons' archive

It was in 1988 that I played a small part in a rescue operation for Jack and Ray's remarkable archive, much of which was stored in 'Room 11' – a room in the cottage which unknown to me for a decade was the depository for the extraordinary mass of documents that Jack and Ray had managed to get shipped out of South Africa in 1965. I first entered this Aladdin's cave in July 1987 when the distinguished South African historian, Shula Marks, came on a visit to me and I took her to see Jack and Ray. It was clear that the documents were suffering from the depredations of damp, rats, termites and silver fish and that there was a need for something to be done. Shula persuaded the Swedish International Aid Agency (SIDA), which was the major financier of the ANC at that time, to pay for an archivist to come and sort the papers in Lusaka before shipping them to Sweden for storage until such time as they could be returned to South Africa. Later in the year Jack and Ray built the archive room – an extension of Jack's study – as a place for the storage and sorting of the papers.

I spent a good deal of time in the early months of 1988 helping Annika van Gylswyk to sort the papers. Annika was a Swedish archivist who had lived and worked in South Africa for many years with her Dutch/South African husband before her deportation from the country. I've always remembered how, when we were doing an initial inspection of the papers in 'Room 11', Annika said, 'I'm sure there's a rat in this box', and a rat jumped out! Sorting the papers, which included documents relating to the history of the ANC, the SACP, the Food and Canning Workers Union, the Trade Unions Congress of South Africa (TUCSA), the South African Congress of Trade Unions (SACTU), as well as the historical material collected for Jack and Ray's various books, was an education in itself. The documents were packed and shipped to the Scandinavian Institute of African Studies at Uppsala in Sweden where Annika continued to work on them for several years. She returned to Lusaka to organise a further shipment to Sweden in May 1990. They were eventually returned to South Africa and ceremonially handed over to the library of the University of Cape Town in February 1995.

Returning home

At the time that we were sorting the papers we had no way of knowing when apartheid would come to an end - as late as 1988 Jack was uncertain that he would live to return home. It was on 2 February 1990 that FW de Klerk announced the un-banning of the ANC and the SACP. Oliver Tambo had had a stroke a few months previously and the leadership of the ANC was in some disarray. Although Walter Sisulu, Govan Mbeki, and most of the other Robben Island prisoners had visited Lusaka in January and had told the members of the ANC to prepare to return home, the exile leadership seemed to be uncertain how to respond to de Klerk's announcement. Some leaders, such as Chris Hani, were deeply suspicious of the South African government's intentions. Members of the national executive were sent around to tell members at branch meetings that they should not think that they would be returning home soon. Pallo Jordan was sent to deliver this message to the Roma Branch meeting, which took place at UNZA. After he had spoken, Jack, who was in the week of his 83rd birthday and was one of the most highly respected, if not the most highly respected, members of the ANC in Lusaka, stood up and said: 'I've been in exile for twenty-five years. Nobody can come here and tell me that I'm not going home. I'm going home!'. With that he walked out of the meeting – I know because I met him just after he walked out and I never saw him so angry. He was followed by Ray and Reg September, but he refused their offer of a lift home. In the end Reg had to get out of the car and walk back to Roma with him. It was probably as a result of this intervention, and some lobbying by Ray, that the ANC, which had real security concerns about their return, changed its mind and announced in mid February that Jack and Ray would be the first exiled members of the organisation to return officially to South Africa.

They left Lusaka for their first visit home on 2 March 1990 – this was the day after Nelson Mandela, with Winnie, had arrived in Lusaka to meet the ANC on his first overseas trip since his release from Pollsmoor Prison on 11 February. Jack and Ray travelled on this occasion with their daughter, Mary, who had come to help them make preparations to leave. I went to the airport with them and it was only then that I realised that this was a media event. I was allowed to go out to the plane with them and it was a great privilege to be able to carry Jack's briefcase up the steps and into the aircraft – it was also the only time that I have ever appeared, or will ever appear, on BBC television news! Their arrival in South Africa did not go entirely without incident as they were held up at the airport for several hours, but they were eventually allowed in though labelled as 'prohibited immigrants' and given permits for ninety days. In an interview on Focus on Africa that evening Jack indicated his impression that, judging from their reception, little had changed. They were away in Cape Town for three months during which they also travelled to Namibia to attend the independence celebrations as honoured guests.

Oxfam buying 260 Zambezi Road

I'm not quite sure where the idea that Oxfam should buy 250 Zambezi Road originated. I have a feeling that it may have begun with me though I suppose it was a fairly obvious idea and several people including Mike Edwards' successor, Pushpanath, now in Oxford, and Robin Palmer, were involved in developing it. It was probably never going to be straightforward because Zambia's stringent foreign exchange control regulations made it very difficult to get permission to take even small quantities of money out of the country. It would have been much simpler if the end of apartheid had come a couple of years later – among the first actions of the Movement for Multiparty Democracy (MMD) government that came to power in October 1991 was the liberalisation of these regulations. As Robin has indicated (chapter 12) the purchase became very complicated because the French Canadian Governor of the Bank of Zambia agreed under pressure to make an exception and to allow the payment to be remitted, but he insisted that the payment must be brought into Zambia.

This was always going to involve heavy bank charges, but it was also predictable from the beginning that, if the money remained in Zambia for any length of time, it might be affected by the then frequent devaluations of the kwacha. Oxfam made its payment to Zambia after one devaluation and then the money became stuck in the bank, which, at one stage, was threatening to remit the money in instalments over ten years. In the end there was a delay of several months during which further devaluations occurred. This was doubly painful for the Simons as the delay made it difficult for them to buy a house in Cape Town and the eventual payment in foreign exchange was less than it should have been. In the end Oxfam made up the difference, but only after some distressing correspondence, phone calls, and visits to lawyers – and, I see from my own letters to the Simons in their papers, at least one visit by myself to the Oxfam's finance director. There were times when I regretted the fact that I had become an intermediary between the Simons and Oxfam, but I received some encouragement at the time from mutual friends with business experience like Simon Zukas and the late Theo Bull, and I think that, in the end, Oxfam was the right buyer. It has made good use of the plot and the houses on it for nearly twenty years and its concerns with such issues as drought and poverty are close to Jack and Ray's concerns.

Dramatic events in Lusaka, June – July 1990

After their public return home in March, Jack and Ray returned to Lusaka to pack up in May and left for the second and last time in July 1990. Before leaving, they wrote to Kenneth Kaunda to thank him for his support, saying:

> *We came here as exiles and return with the status, rights and obligations of South African citizens, free of all special restrictions. This is an amazing turnabout, which we owe to the great democratic movement at home, international support, and the enormous contribution by you, your Excellency, and the people of Zambia. You have done much to make possible the triumph of reason and a higher morality that transcends the limits of self-seeking expediency.*[8]

They had originally intended to leave on 1 July but their departure was delayed for a week by dramatic events in Lusaka. It was on 25 June that UNZA students who had planned to march on parliament to protest against the removal of mealie meal subsidies were turned back by police on the Great East Road and decided to take the revolution to the compounds, starting with Kaunda Square, Kalingalinga and Mutendere. I was at a meeting at the Institute of African Studies that morning and as I saw the students marching down to Kaunda Square I thought that their chances of rousing the population were slim. How wrong I was! Riots and targeted attacks on state shops had soon broken out all over the place. I had a distinguished American historian staying with me and, after one somewhat scary encounter with stone-throwing youths and gun-toting paramilitary police on the Great East Road near Munali, he could not leave the country fast enough. He demanded that he should be taken to the airport at seven the next morning in time for a five pm flight. I refused to leave so early but gave in at about 10am and then decided to take him via 250 Zambezi Road so that I could check on Jack and Ray who were preparing for their departure. I have never forgotten the way in which Jack took the historian to task for his lack of interest in contemporary social events. He asked him what kind of historian he was and, taking out his notebook, he recorded his name and address, as if intending to report him to a higher authority. I got the historian to the airport in good time, but only just managed to get home myself before the road was closed again by another outbreak of rioting.

That was a very exciting week with the riots soon followed by the one-man coup of Captain Luchembe and, I think, the announcement that there would be a referendum on the one-party state in October. Later in the month

---

8   Ray Alexander Simons, *All my life and all my strength*, edited by Raymond Suttner, Johannesburg, STE Publishers, 2004, 348.

there was the Garden House meeting out of which the MMD emerged. The referendum was later abandoned as there was clearly no need for it. It seemed somehow suitable that Jack and Ray should be leaving at this dramatic juncture – there was little doubt that the political change in Zambia came about as a direct consequence of the end of apartheid and of the liberation struggle, which had provided some kind of justification, or excuse, for the one-party state and other limitations on political freedom.

On the morning of their final departure, 9 July 1990, I remember Ray taking me around the garden and giving me instructions which I should pass on to Oxfam on the maintenance of the trees, especially the grapevine behind Johan's house. In the five years that I remained in Lusaka I was a regular visitor to the Oxfam offices at 250 Zambezi Road during the regimes of Pushpanath and Lucy Muyoyeta, but I'm not sure that I was able to carry out Ray's wishes about the trees. On a visit to Lusaka in August 2005 I did make a belated effort to carry out her instructions. With the help of my friends, Geoffrey and Michael Mee, and with the encouragement of Oxfam's Country Representative, Ric Goodman, I recruited an Afrikaner viticulturalist, a Mr Botha, to prune the vine – for the first time in many years. I hope that it is now bearing more fruit. I also discussed with Ric the possibility of putting up a plaque to commemorate the lives of Jack and Ray and the part played by them and their house in the liberation struggle. I had some correspondence with Susie and Robin Palmer about the house at that time and it was, perhaps, Susie's nostalgic writing about 250 Zambezi Road, as well as her untimely death, which triggered the collection of reminiscences to which this is a contribution.

Jack lived in South African for long enough to take part in the first democratic elections in April 1994 and died on 22 July 1995 in his eighty-ninth year. Ray lived long enough to celebrate her ninetieth birthday in December 2003 and died in Cape Town on 12 September 2004.

The Story of a House

Jack & Ray Simons going into exile, Zambezi Valley, Zambia, 1965

Ray & Jack leaving for South Africa, March 1990

A House in Zambia

Hugh Macmillan, 1990

Cde Jack & Cde Ray voting on election day in South Africa, April 1994

3. 'ENTABENI': A HOME IN LUSAKA AWAY FROM HOME

Tanya Barben

My first visit to my parents in Lusaka

I visited Lusaka for the first time in December 1967, to spend the first of many university vacations or periods of annual leave visiting my parents in our new home in the 'township' of Roma. It was comforting to see that, just like our former Cape Town home on the lower slopes of Table Mountain, our house in Zambia bore the appellation, 'Entabeni'. Perhaps 250 Zambezi Road was not 'under the mountain', but it certainly was 'a place of refuge' for many, and one where the Simons family could re-assemble on occasion.

My parents and I corresponded regularly during the 25 years of their exile from South Africa. Thousands of letters passed between me in Cape Town and them en route to Zambia and from Manchester, London and Lusaka (or, as in the case of my mother, from any of the world destinations she visited while undertaking her unionizing activities). They wrote glowingly of Lusaka and Zambia, and were very excited to announce in August 1965 that they had bought a hillside plot (2¼ acres) in a semi-rural area. The Edmundses were our nearest neighbours, two plots away, and they had a cow, horses, and ducks as well as the usual cats and dogs. The design of the house was a combined effort, we all threw our ideas into a virtual hat – I remember asking for a fireplace and an L-shaped kitchen. Of course its construction was not without problems and my mother had to hurry away from England to whip the architect and the builder into line and to plant some fruit trees, the genesis of what was later to develop into an extremely productive orchard.

Mom and Dad moved into our new home at the end of 1967. I remember Dad's complaining about the heat and the 'goggas': scorpions, houseflies, flying ants, mosquitoes and beetles – this was before flyscreens were installed on all doors and windows - and wondering whether the fridge would arrive before my sister, Mary, and I did on our first visit. Perhaps it is that visit that I remember most vividly. The trip there was, in itself, an adventure for me. We travelled second class by train through a hot Karroo, a hotter Botswana and across the then Rhodesia. We were accompanied by the family dog, Brennie, who was initially confined to the indignity of the guard's van where she was humiliated by a caged monkey who pelted her with banana and orange peels. I was allowed to take her for walks every time the train stopped for any length of time at a siding or remote station. After the second or third day Brennie was permitted to join us in our compartment during the day. Amid mounting excitement we crossed the mighty Zambezi River and saw the Victoria Falls early in the morning and then waited in Zambia for the immigration and customs formalities to be completed. Brennie became very restless, wagging her tail and yapping excitedly in her doggy way. We stuck our heads out of the window, to see in the distance among the many people milling about the railroad a familiar figure sitting on an African drum surrounded by parcels. Our mother had come to give us a warm African welcome! Brennie had remembered her and heard her calls. Mom was quite peeved that the dog, though much loved, and not her daughters had responded to her cries.

Many, many hours later, after sunset, we arrived at Lusaka's station. The doors were jammed so we had to squeeze our luggage plus dog and later ourselves through the train's windows. Among the throngs of people milling about the platform was our father. After more joyous greetings we were whisked away in the familiar blue and white Opel Rekord through the grid plan streets of central Lusaka and along the darkness of the Great East Road to our new home. Too excited and happy to do much more than rejoice at our reunion and marvel at the brilliant starry sky arcing above us, we went to sleep in our new home to be awoken, awash in an unfamiliar heat and humidity, by the incessant buzzing, sawing and chirping of a multitude of insects both within and outside the house.

The grounds had to be explored. They appeared to be vast, covered with indigenous vegetation and that vegetation itself teeming with caterpillars, worms and army ants. Every few feet I saw huge chongololos, those millipedes so evident in Central Africa, crawling over the orange earth and chameleons camouflaged in trees, lazily swivelling their eyes and feasting on those very pesky insects that wheeled, swarmed and crawled about. This fecundity of the vegetation and its attendant insect life as well as the friendliness of the Zambian people is perhaps what I remember most vividly about my second home. Much had to be done: a lawn was to be planted in front of the house and the huge back area needed to be cleared. All would be accomplished over the many years that followed. I remember assisting with the planting and watering of grass and watching my father eradicate bagworms infesting a tree by using paraffin – and burning not only the trees but also his eyebrows - 'Don't tell your mother', he urged us.

The house itself was a delight with its beautifully polished parquet floors, a wonderful sandstone fireplace – I remember all of us helping Dad choose a present for Mom in the form of a magnificent copper fire screen from the then Zaire – two bathrooms and a lovely, easy to use L-shaped kitchen with a large pantry. Remembered paintings hung on the walls. There were bookshelves everywhere on which could be found many much-loved and familiar titles, although the bulk of our home library was donated to the newly established University of Zambia, where my father was later to be appointed Professor of Sociology. There was so much to see, to do and to wonder at. The first of my twenty odd visits to 250 Zambezi Road was a success. Apart from anything else I was no longer a gypsy, I had a home once more.

In later years

During the following years the house 'grow'd like Topsy'. The kitchen verandah roof was given a ceiling and a cottage was built in 1968 to accommodate Oliver Tambo, that wise, self-effacing giant of a man whose ritual cheek scarifications fascinated me. Although a frequent visitor to the main house, how often he lived in the cottage I do not know. Zola Zembe or Emile aka Archie Sibeko was an occupant, as was Ruth Mompati who became a much-loved friend, the Makiwanes, possibly Todd and Esme Matshikiza, Sholto Cross, and many, many others. Rob and Marion Molteno stayed in the big house for a while until they were able to find alternative quarters. Visitors streamed in through the back door (hardly anyone used the front door which faced Zambezi Road), often stroking the large wooden elephant that stood guard. Some of these included Justin Chimba, a minister in Kenneth Kaunda's cabinet, and his wife, Chris Hani, Harry Chimowitz, Hugh, Monica and John Macmillan and countless, countless others. I shall never forget the slap-slap-bang of the screen door, despite its squeaking hydraulic hinge, every time it was entered or exited. All were welcome and plied with homemade lemon syrup and ever present biscuits.

The cottage increased in size to house both people and a growing archive of papers. A new wing was later added to provide my father with a study and the front verandah was enclosed. Every visit revealed further additions in the form of crops, animals and people. For many years the wonderful, kind, accomplished Gerrard Phiri cleaned the house, oversaw the pots on the stove when asked to, and tended in the garden under intermittent supervision. That garden flourished, despite the heat and the prophecies of drought and flood. Avocado pears, pawpaws, bananas, plantains, mangoes, guavas, citrus varieties, mulberries, Himalayan raspberries, strawberries, okra, litchis, green peppers, green beans, aubergines, courgettes, tomatoes, onions, potatoes, maize, and thick-skinned grapes grew in profusion. The pantry was filled to capacity with preserves, pickles, syrups, jams and marmalades made from the garden produce. There was something so therapeutic about being able to decide on today's meal on the basis of today's harvest. I was able to survive the biting cold of winter mornings thanks to the frisson on hearing the raucous caw of pied crows that I was told (perhaps not accurately) had migrated to our garden from the steppes of central Asia.

Roma expands

Living in a semi-rural environment was a delight, although just as the house grew, so did Roma. The family practice of an evening walk and a longer one on Sunday mornings continued. My father took me across rivers and beside languid pools in which our accompanying dogs paddled. We walked past maize and sugar cane fields, watching small children from nearby N'gombe Village, all of whom seemed to know my Dad, chew the cane, their shiny brown cheeks smeared with its sticky juices. Before long, however, this rural Eden gave way to rampant development. More houses were built, fences and walls erected, and swimming pools excavated. Our overgrown paths were replaced by the tarmac and concrete of Mulungushi Village, and our explorations curtailed somewhat. Before this happened, though, I was able to hire a horse and go riding around Roma and its environs.

In 1973 the plot was subdivided and a house was built for my brother, Johan, who for many years worked in Lusaka. It was into this house that Susie Smith of Oxfam and her dog, Bobby, were to move. Susie was to become as close as a daughter to my parents and a much loved family friend. Her presence was, of course, a great comfort to me, as postal communication was not always satisfactory, and the telephone was more often out of order than working.

The situation in South Africa was never forgotten, neither was our vulnerability on our return from a Zambian visit, as we might well be hounded by the South African Special Branch. It was never a good idea for us to know too much, so often I was sequestered in my bedroom while special visitors were entertained or discussions held. These fears were, of course, realized when Mary and I were 'banned' or restricted in terms of the Internal Security Act, from November 1976 to October 1981. This meant that the visits to Zambia were halted. It was not until June 1982 that I was able to return to find that much had changed, not only in 'Entabeni' but in Lusaka and Zambia. The promises of independence had been somewhat diluted, goods of any description were hard to find and the country was clearly suffering from the South African government's economic reprisals meted out to a state that supported the liberation movements. I always arrived in Zambia with suitcases bursting at the seams filled with supplies – necessities as well as luxuries in some cases.

My parents were ageing. They had devoted most of their lives to the struggle for the liberation of South Africa. They had become the surrogate parents and mentors of people from all over the world who joined the struggle as well as a host of exiles from South Africa and Namibia. Their home was a home for all. Their garden's abundance not only catered for our needs and those of the comrades, but also supplied Lusaka's markets after some shrewd bartering on my mother's part. I was able to visit for only three weeks a year, my precious annual leave, something we all found difficult and unsatisfactory. This became particularly so when I brought my children with me, first as babes in arms and later as restless, energetic and justifiably demanding toddlers who loved nothing more than to grub around in the garden and get thoroughly dirty, much to my mother's consternation and my father's delight. If truth be told, though, they did not really have the time to either parent or grandparent; their days were spent with far more pressing matters. The Macmillans came to the rescue, entertained us, and took us to swimming pools and to visit the even then magnificent Munda Wanga gardens outside Lusaka.

A House in Zambia

My last visit

My last visit to 'Entabeni' took place in November 1989. Jacques, then four, spent his mornings in a play centre at the end of Zambezi Road. Marc, at nineteen months, was kept happily occupied in house and garden. The memory of this visit is somewhat skewed by the fact that the over friendly Jacques was bitten on the face by a dog at the local supermarket. The local doctor patched him up but advised rabies injections because nothing was known about the dog. My parents were remarkably calm, I disgraced myself by fainting in the surgery. My father roamed about the nearby settlements trying to track down the dog, gave this up as a fruitless exercise and then established that the only source of a rabies injection was the ANC medical unit. Poor Jacques had to endure the necessary – and welcome - injections into his stomach tissues, administered on a kitchen table. I must admit that it was with some relief that we returned to South Africa and the sophistication of its private medical services.

My parents return home

Our world was turned rightside up by De Klerk's announcement of the unbanning of the liberation organizations on 2 February 1990. I called my father to give him the astonishing, miraculous news and asked when he planned to come home. This my parents did on 2 March, to a tumultuous welcome, returning to Lusaka in May to pack up their home for a final departure in early July. They brought with them from Lusaka the 'Entabeni' nameplate which was affixed to the outside wall of an apartment in Vredehoek, one of the City Bowl suburbs nestling on the lower slopes of Table Mountain. Their home was once again both under the mountain and a place of refuge.

Entabeni

Tanya Barben, friend Nyosa & father Jack Simons outside 250 Zambezi Road, 1982

A House in Zambia

Jack leaving 250 Zambezi Road for the last time, July 1990

Ray & Jack outside 250 Zambezi Road, 1990

4. OXFAM IN SOUTHERN AFRICA IN THE 1980s

Peter Wiles

My memories of 250 Zambezi Road are regrettably quite limited. This is partly due to *anno domini* and also due to the fact that I was Regional Representative for South Africa, Namibia and Lesotho during part of this time, so my visits to Lusaka were limited.

Oxfam's work in Southern Africa

Before turning to those memories, it may be worth putting Oxfam's work in Southern Africa during the early 1980s into some kind of context. I returned from India in late 1979 and took over the Southern Africa desk from Bernadette Prat who sadly died later in Zaire (now DRC).[1] I found myself working with Susie Smith and both of us were managed by Michael Behr. With the arrival of Zimbabwean independence in 1980, I remember that both Susie and I were miffed that Michael decided to go off and open a new programme in Zimbabwe, as we were both looking forward to working with him.

During the first years of the 1980s we undertook a substantial re-engineering of the Southern Africa programme. Prior to 1980, the funded projects in South Africa and Namibia had been kept quiet. Many of them did not appear on the published grants lists and Oxfam said nothing publicly about its work there. This dangerous, unaccountable and untenable situation was quickly recognised by Paddy Coulter, arriving as the new Press Officer.

Other forces of change were also at work. We realised that the SADCC (Southern African Development Coordination Conference) group of countries plus South Africa and Namibia had to be treated as one region in a coordinated way. What Oxfam did in one country affected what it did in another. The liberation movements were increasingly asking Oxfam what we were doing in South Africa and why. The Anti-Apartheid Movement in the UK was also doing the same. During a visit to Mozambique in the late

---

1 Sadly, a seemingly disproportionate number of people who worked on Oxfam's Southern Africa programme have died before their time – Joan Wright, Michael Behr, Odhiambo Anacleti and now Susie Smith herself.

1970s Oxfam's director Brian Walker had been rebuffed by the FRELIMO leadership because of our South African involvement.

During 1980 or 1981 I undertook a review of how the South Africa/ Namibia/ Lesotho programmes were managed. Susie, Michael Behr and I travelled down to Lesotho by car to discuss the work with the then Field Director, Joe Parsons. Given the sensitivities of the programmes and the need to keep good communication between the programme, Oxfam HQ and the neighbouring countries, it was decided to close the Lesotho office and manage the programme from Oxford with a Regional Representative travelling three months of the year. At the same time we appointed a black South African field worker, Alex Mbatha, who worked with us under the auspices of the Southern Africa Catholic Bishops' Conference.

Michael and Susie persuaded me to take the new job which I did from 1982 to 1984. Those two years were the most intensive and stimulating of what I loosely call my career, coinciding with a period of unprecedented political activity in South Africa.

We strengthened the Southern Africa programme by having regional meetings every six months. These were, I believe, effective in developing some coherence in Oxfam's work. Oxfam's first African Country Representatives, Odhiambo Anacleti (Tanzania) and Peter Nyoni (Zimbabwe) played a key role in our discussions and their wise words were often able to calm the passions of us Northerners.

A new policy for Southern Africa

These meetings also provided the vehicle by which we developed a new policy for Southern Africa. After consultation in South Africa and Namibia, a document was drafted that was scrutinised and re-drafted at a major meeting in Harare in 1981, attended by an incoming Overseas Director David Bryer, the chair of the Africa Committee, Sir Frank Lloyd, and Brian Walker, Oxfam's Director. The paper was subsequently approved by Oxfam's Council in June 1982.

The most important elements of this policy were:
1. A clear recognition that apartheid and the illegal occupation of Namibia were major underlying causes of impoverishment and conflict throughout the region;

2. The need for Oxfam to develop a public information programme about Southern Africa;
3. The need to have relationships with the Southern African liberation movements;
4. A restatement of the need to take a regional view of work in that part of Africa.

In some ways, point 2 was the most important for Oxfam. It cleared the way for the development of information and education work on the region which gradually developed during the 1980s until the debacle with the Charity Commissioners in 1990. Paddy Coulter kicked this work off with a paper called 'Bridging the Communications Gap on Southern Africa'. This work was led by a tightly knit working group in Oxford, the Southern Africa Working Group (SAWG).

A high priority was given to educating Oxfam's supporters and we saw this as information work that reached areas that the Anti-apartheid Movement was not reaching. The 1985 Gilbert Murray lecture in Oxford was to be given by Dr Allan Boesak, a fiery critic of apartheid. He was not able to get a visa and his place was taken by one of our closest partners in South Africa, Fr S'mangaliso Mkhatshwa, Secretary General of the Southern Africa Bishops Conference. Fr Mkhatshwa made a marvellous speech to a packed Oxford Union debating hall.[2]

Most crucially, the ground was laid for Oxfam to withdraw its bank accounts from Barclays Bank because of the latter's involvement in South Africa and Namibia. This campaign was a major process in itself, partly because most of the honorary treasurers of Oxfam groups were Barclays Bank managers. Another high-level working group chaired by a former Oxfam director, Sir Lesley Kirkley, produced the paper that went to Oxfam's Council. In fact, the major protagonist who pushed the issue through was Joel Joffe, now Lord Joffe. Until the afternoon of the Council vote on 23 November 1985 we did not know which way the decision would go, and Paddy Coulter and his colleagues in the Press Office were standing by with 'Yes' press releases and 'No' press releases. I remember the yell

---

2   Subsequent events with Dr Boesak meant that it was fortuitous for Oxfam that he was unable to give the speech.

that went up when the Yes vote came through. A few months later, Barclays withdrew from South Africa and Namibia.[3]

The detention of the Mbathas

Probably the two key events to mention during this period were the detention of Alex Mbatha and his family and the launch of the first Oxfam anti-apartheid campaign. Alex, his wife Khosi and their three year old daughter Dudu were arrested on 22 October 1981. Dudu was released quickly but little was heard about Alex and Khosi. On 22 January 1982, Oxfam, Catholic Fund for Overseas Development (CAFOD) and the British Council of Churches held a vigil at the South African embassy in London, starting exactly three months to the hour since the Mbathas were arrested. Amongst those showing support on the pavement in Trafalgar Square was Joanna Lumley, the actress. This was the first time Oxfam had raised its head publicly in relation to apartheid. Alex and Khosi were released on 14 April 1982 after 175 days in detention. They subsequently gave a moving talk in Oxfam House on their experiences.

The first Oxfam anti-apartheid campaign

The first Oxfam campaign on South Africa, called 'The Poverty of Apartheid – poverty in the midst of plenty', was led by John Clark, head of campaigns, who later worked with the World Bank. It was designed to place Oxfam squarely in the middle of the anti-apartheid struggle, working from a poverty perspective.

Security issues

Security issues were a thread that ran through our work, both for Oxfam staff and for our partners, often not without humour. As Mike Edwards mentions in chapter 8, the liberation movements had code names, Doctors, Nurses and the Industrial Health Tribunal. In South Africa I was known to some as Fr William. The meeting Susie, Michael Behr and I had with Joe Parsons in Lesotho, mentioned above, took place by a waterfall in the mountains to minimise the likelihood of bugging.

---

3   One of the practical arguments against moving from Barclays, was the possible disruption it might cause to Oxfam's bank transfers all over the world and the cost of the change. In fact, the change to National Westminster went smoothly and was less expensive than expected, partly due to Barclays playing a decent game and not taking umbrage.

Susie Smith's role

Susie played a major role in the development of Oxfam's work in Southern Africa, bringing her strong compassion and intellect to bear on all the issues we faced. She took over somewhat moribund projects in Zambia and Malawi and developed a progressive new programme. She also developed substantial and sensitive contacts with the liberation movements based in Lusaka. Susie, along with 250 Zambezi Road, was at the centre of our efforts to respond effectively to the challenges of Southern Africa. She was analysing and feeling the impact of apartheid through her contacts with the Southern African liberation movements and the suffering of Angolan and Namibian refugees in Zambia.

I found myself in the odd situation, once or twice a year, of getting off a South African Airways plane from Johannesburg at Lusaka airport and meeting some of the comrades who were keen to have news from their homeland and see up-to-date copies of the *Rand Daily Mail*. It felt an odd privilege to be in this position and it was to Susie's credit that she was able to establish the credibility and trust required to enable these meetings to happen.

Oxfam's work in South Africa was recognised with David Bryer's invitation to Nelson Mandela's inauguration in 1994. I was always sad that Oxfam seemed to fumble the ball with its programme in South Africa after apartheid ended.[4] However it was good to see the fiftieth anniversary of the programme celebrated in 2006. In that year Oxfam's current Director, Barbara Stocking, went to South Africa to celebrate fifty years of Oxfam working in South Africa. She was on a phone-in and was rather nervous beforehand because of her lack of local knowledge, but it consisted of a lot of people ringing in to celebrate the work Oxfarm had supported in the apartheid years - standing in solidarity with people. So she found the phone-in hugely enjoyable.

4　An answer to Peter's query of why Oxfam failed to build on its 'capital' of 250 Zambezi Road emerged during the creation of this collection. The first in-country Representative appointed was someone who was new to Oxfam and new to South Africa, and so knew nothing of Oxfam's history with the ANC in exile, nor was there a manager who saw the need to fill those gaps.

A House in Zambia

Peter Wiles in Mbatha protest outside South African Embassy, London, January 1982

Oxfam in Southern Africa

Oxfam in South Africa poster, 1980s

A House in Zambia

Book cover Front Line Africa by Susanna Smith, 1990

5. OXFAM'S SUPPORT TO THE ANC IN ZAMBIA IN THE 1980s

Robin Palmer

One of the many interesting things about this collection has been the way in which it has thrown up new questions as successive contributions have come in, and as the contributors have engaged in correspondence with each other. For example, in January 2008, in response to Peter Wiles' piece, Hugh Macmillan asked:

1. *Can he or someone not say more than has been said about Oxfam aid to the ANC - disguised as doctors and nurses as they may have been?*
2. *What sort of aid did Oxfam give to the ANC and when?*
3. *Did they provide any help for the ANC farm near Lusaka? - it may not have needed any help as it was generously funded by SIDA.*

Hugh adds that it was called Chongela Farm and was set up in 1978. It was only then that the ANC got permission to buy a farm and it was funded fairly lavishly by SIDA. It was run as a commercial farm employing Zambian labour and produced meat, maize and vegetables to supply ANC people in Lusaka and in the camps in Angola. At one point when there was a mealie meal shortage in Zambia, the ANC was refused permission to send maize to Angola.

So I set about trying to find answers to those questions.

A major constraint, Peter Wiles notes, is that the ANC did not have a humanitarian wing which Oxfam could have funded under charity rules, and it is his recollection that Oxfam did not give any direct financial aid to the ANC in Zambia or anywhere else during his time (1980-88).

Technically, Peter is correct, but Susie Smith initiated a way of providing small amounts of humanitarian funding to the ANC indirectly, and this was continued by her successors Mike Edwards and Pushpanath. It seems reasonable to assume that this initiative might have been a by-product of Susie becoming a tenant of Jack and Ray Simons at 250 Zambezi Road and the personal and professional relationships that developed from that, which are captured elsewhere in this collection. For example, on 3 June 1981,

Susie wrote to Peter Wiles, 'I believe there is interesting, small-scale work we could assist [the ANC] with... For the time being, I shall just keep a friendly line open.' Hugh Macmillan notes (5 May 2008) that he found;

> A file in the Oxfam archives which indicates that the connection began in 1982 and the initial link was made through Susie by Wolfie Kodesh, a member of the treasury department and a great fund-raiser and general fixer. Money was provided for Chongela farm in Zambia, a farm in Angola, a minibus in Botswana, and also for projects in Tanzania.

Mike Edwards (4 February 2008) recalls that:

> Yes, we supported humanitarian assistance projects for both the ANC and SACTU (the South African Congress of Trade Unions) and also for SWAPO (the South West Africa People's Organisation) throughout my time in Lusaka (1984-88). I was a regular visitor to Chongela Farm outside the city, to various safe houses and the ANC office where Thabo Mbeki worked as ADC to Oliver Tambo.
>
> The assistance consisted of things like mattresses and cooking pots for newly-arriving refugees, and irrigation equipment for the farm, and I think some help with school textbooks and the like for the children of SWAPO members. It was never a lot of money though - they didn't need it.
>
> The only thing I can't recall was whether the grants were paid directly or through an intermediary.

In fact they were paid through an intermediary, CUSO (originally Canadian University Service Overseas), with whom Oxfam shared an office in downtown Lusaka.

Mike notes that he inherited this work from Susie 'under whom it was already well-established'. The Simons were never a formal go-between, 'but obviously their connections helped to make the way for introductions, etc'.

Mike's successor Pushpanath recalls (4 February 2008) that:

> Yes, humanitarian support was given – always the intermediary was CUSO – and I continued to keep a brief on this from 1988. As a matter of fact it is our work with Doctors (ANC) and Nurses

(SWAPO) that brought a number of Oxfams and CUSO together as a precursor to Oxfam International.

We started to look at what each of us did with the doctors and nurses and also consequently what kind of regional work. This was the first time the Oxfams started talking to one other - it started before I came on the scene - and the first inter-Oxfam regional work started in Lusaka and covered Southern and East Africa.

Another initiative was that we as donors initiated what we called confession sessions - explaining the muck and the muddle of what we did; chalking out joint work; drawing what these days we would call lessons and best practices. It was so much fun and we laughed so much and built a good working relationship and plans.

Details of Oxfam's indirect funding have been obtained from some of the project files, thanks to the efforts of Oxfam's Archivist, Rosie Dodd. In the 1980s these are the grants that she found listed made to CUSO, Lusaka:

1981/82
ZAM 066. Training workshop on humanitarian settlement   £2,000

1983/84
ZAM 067. Irrigation equipment for agricultural training   £7,578
Furniture and equipment   £4,773 (this followed a refusal to pay airfares)

1985/86
ZAM 067. Borehole, piping and pump for refugee agricultural project   £11,967

Pre-school crèche and educational materials for ANC members' children   £2,000

ZAM 083. Domestic equipment for newly arrived refugees   £5,029

1986/87
ZAM 083. Purchase of seeds for refugee agricultural development programme   £6,450

ZAM 120. School fees for ANC members' children   £1,711

Rosie adds that there are then no more specific references to CUSO, but in 1987/88 a new line emerges that might be relevant:

1987/88
To various agencies helping with refugees   £22,539
1988/89
To various agencies: humanitarian work with refugees   £36,477
1989/90
To various agencies: humanitarian work with refugees   £30,809

There were similar levels of funding to SWAPO,[1] which included support to SWAPO's Nyango Camp in the Western Province.[2] To some degree Oxfam's fingerprints were removed in these files,[3] but not entirely. Here, for example, is CUSO Regional Programs Director John van Mossel writing to the ANC's Treasurer-General in Lusaka on 22 October 1986:

> *This is to forward to you a cheque in the amount of K47,396.53 [£6,450] being the amount transferred to CUSO by Oxfam-UK. This represents Oxfam-UK's contribution to the Chongela package, involving non-government support and EEC matching grants. This amount is particularly ear marked for the seeds component of the package... I do hope that the crucial work at Chongela farm continues and proves increasingly productive, meeting the ever expanding requirements of the ANC.*

The ANC's Treasurer-General, T.T. Nkobi, replied on 31 October 1986, acknowledging receipt of the cheque:

> *We wish to express our heartfelt gratitude to CUSO and OXFAM UK for the continued good cooperation that exists between the ANC and the said Organisations.*

---

1   In files ZAM 061, 064, 083, 087, 091, 121 and 122.
2   Some of the funding went through Socialist Solidarity of Belgium in order to unlock EEC grants.
3   My thanks to my former Oxfam colleague David Walker, a South African, for looking through these files on my behalf while I was temporarily incapacitated with a fractured hip.

Oxfam's Support to the ANC in Zambia in the 1980s

Interestingly, Chris Dammers, who in 1984 succeeded Peter Wiles as the Oxford-based manager of Oxfam's programme inside South Africa,[4] recalls (5 February 2008) that he was not a great supporter of this kind of funding. He explains why:

Actually I was quite sceptical about this 'solidarity funding' because, as Mike Edwards points out, the 'health workers' (ANC and SWAPO) had more substantial donors, and these grants did potentially jeopardize Oxfam's much larger programmes within South Africa and Namibia - though they probably also generated some positive messages about Oxfam to people inside.

Oxfam was unusual in pursuing both external and internal funding, which was generally considered too risky, though effectively we got away with it.

Mike Edwards adds (5 February 2008) this interesting coda to Chris' view on funding:

When I was part of a donors' visit to the (ANC) Chongela farm, we were taken to see the irrigation equipment that we had helped to purchase (along with the prize pigs, nick-named Maggie and P.W.Botha), only to find that each agency thought it had funded the same piece of equipment by itself!

Solidarity funding - those were the days!

---

4   His title was Field Director, later Regional Representative, for Southern Africa a post he held from 1984-88. He says that 90% of his work was on South Africa.

A House in Zambia

Oxfam Southern Africa regional meeting Livingstone,1987: Bob Gibson (Zaire),Joan Wright (South Africa), Chris Dammers (South Africa), Lucy Muyoyeta (Zambia), Ann Wigglesworth (Mozambique), Robin Palmer (regional), Mike Edwards (Zambia), Michael Behr (ex-Zimbabwe

Five contributors outside Oxfam House, May 2008: Peter Wiles, Martin Kalungu-Banda, Sue Cavanna, Robin Palmer, Victor Pelekamoyo

PART TWO:

THE OXFAM REPRESENTATIVES IN ZAMBIA

6. SUSIE SMITH (1980-84)

I visited Zambia for the first time in seventeen years in October 2004. I was surprised and delighted that quite a few of the Oxfam staff there were interested to know more about the history of our 250 Zambezi Road compound in particular, and Oxfam's history in Zambia in general.

So, as promised, this is my personal account of a period in the life of this compound in eastern Lusaka, from 1980 to 1984. It's about the place, the people who made it, and the Oxfam history surrounding it. I am writing it not only for the current staff, but also in memory of the people in this story, so many of whom, it now strikes me, have died. My aim has been to write my bit then pass it on to others connected with the place to add their recollections.[1]

Oxfam moves its 'Central Africa' office to Lusaka in 1979

The nomenclature itself is instructive. I started as Oxfam's 'Field Director' for Zambia and Malawi at the end of 1979, taking over from Martyn Young [2] who did the same job but based in Blantyre in neighbouring Malawi. Martyn died back in the UK in the mid 1980s, he couldn't have been more than forty.

Oxfam moved the office (for Malawi and Zambia) from Blantyre to Lusaka in mid to late 1979 – the reasons are important. Michael Behr [3] had become the 'Senior Field Secretary' for Africa and with Peter Wiles and later David Bryer he had led a move for Oxfam to get more engaged with the liberation politics and aspirations of Southern Africa, in particular, of Zimbabwe/Rhodesia (as it was then known), of Namibia, and of South Africa. Michael's role is well described in Maggie Black's account of

---

1   Susie wrote this in late 2004, revising it in June 2005.
2   Martyn had been an Oxfam 'Regional Organiser', that is fundraiser and local representative, in the south of England previous to moving to be Deputy Field Director under Colin McKone based in Malawi, later to become the Field Director. He is fondly remembered by the ex-Oxfam staff in Zambia, as well as by me and his friend dating back to Malawi days who later joined Oxfam - Nick Stockton.
3   Michael was one of Oxfam's truly outstanding leaders; visionary, compassionate, insightful, gentle as well as stubborn, funny, irreverent, supportive and gifted - and totally committed to Oxfam's cause. I, and many others, miss him immensely.

Oxfam's history, *A Cause for Our Times*.[4] Michael died in 2003.

Michael himself had moved down to Salisbury to start an Oxfam programme from within Zimbabwe/Rhodesia in 1979, (previous to that, Martyn and before him Colin McKone had supported work in Zimbabwe/Rhodesia from Blantyre), and Martyn was asked to move the Zambia/Malawi office to Lusaka. It was felt that in the world of Frontline States [5] politics which Oxfam was trying to adjust to, Blantyre was not only very far away from the action (Malawi was never a Frontline State, rather it was a dictatorship politically aligned with South Africa), but was also unlikely to be a place where one could analyse the currents of thinking and be a part of the networks Oxfam needed. Most importantly though, we chose Lusaka because Zambia was a strong Frontline State which had suffered considerable economic downturn due to the war in Rhodesia and international sanctions against the Smith regime; and because the exiled HQ of the ANC was there (their office was in the back alley behind Cairo Road, very close by our office) as well as a SWAPO office (their main exile HQ was in Luanda) and the important UN Institute for Namibia (UNIN), which worked to establish future government policies (on land, fishing, education, health etc) and train a future civil service for an independent Namibia – a prospect which seemed very far off at that time.

Martyn duly opened the Oxfam office in the CUSA (Credit Union and Savings Association of Zambia – an organisation which no longer exists) building at the South End of Cairo Road, within walking distance of Soweto Market where we used to go and enjoy lunch sometimes. His first staff hire was Martin Malitino Daka,[6] the office messenger, and then Dorothy Chikula, office secretary.

Shortly after I came, I got permission to hire a driver (most of the project visits I had to undertake were a minimum of ten hours' drive away), and Wilson Kaonza joined us from the Austrian Embassy. We stayed as a staff of four for all the time I was there - the rapid expansion of Oxfam's international offices happened later in the 1980s.

---

4   *A Cause for Our Times: Oxfam the first 50 years* by Maggie Black, published by Oxfam, Oxford, 1992. This book is long but very interesting reading for anyone who wants to understand Oxfam's past and the nature of the organisation. I hope it is in every international Oxfam office library.

5   So-called because they were, politically if not all physically, on the front line between apartheid South Africa and independent anti-apartheid Africa.

6   His name was actually Malitino Matulino Daka; clearly he and Susie agreed on 'Martin' as an anglicized version of Matulino.

Susie Smith

Finding 250 Zambezi Road

For the first few months I was in Zambia I couldn't find a satisfactory place to live. As I was living alone, I needed a place where I wouldn't feel too isolated and where I could safely keep the Oxfam vehicle (I think we took the big step of expanding to a two vehicle operation in Mike Edwards' time). At that time, Lusaka was affected by an armed crime wave. It was thought that the pre-existing crime levels had suddenly been given a boost by a sudden glut of automatic rifles (AK 47s) and ammunition which the destitute ZIPRA[7] guerrillas had sold, allegedly often just for food and shelter, in the south of the country as the armed part of Zimbabwe's independence struggle was coming to an end.

Through David Saunders (then Oxfam's medical advisor in Zimbabwe who, with Michael and his successor Peter Nyoni did a fantastic job of resuscitating the ruined hospitals and health services destroyed by war in Zimbabwe's 'communal areas'), I met the late Harry and Marjorie Chimowitz (white socialist exiles from Zimbabwe and later South Africa who had set up home in Lusaka – they were great friends to me and to Michael Holman of the Financial Times who lived in their garden cottage) who introduced me to their lifelong friends Jack and Ray Simons, because the Simons were looking for a lodger for one of the three houses in their Zambezi Road compound.[8]

I went round to inspect the property on offer, and it was by far the most suitable place I had yet found. It was secure, and there were other people living in the same plot. At that time, I knew nothing about the owners except that they seemed friendly and interesting people and they were happy for me to bring my fierce-looking but friendly dog, Bobby [9] (also, of course, dead). And so I moved in, probably in late 1980.

---

7   ZIPRA, the Zimbabwe People's Revolutionary Army, was the armed wing of Joshua Nkomo's ZAPU party.
8   Harry and Marjorie had a wide circle of interesting friends and were particularly hospitable people – Michael Holman and I met again recently in Pretoria and spoke of those interesting evenings where we would sit with Joe Slovo, Mac and Zarina Maharaj and their little son Cabral, Simon and Cynthia Zukas, Bente Lorenz, and many others, discussing the state of the world.
9   Friendly to everyone except, unaccountably, my Canadian friend Barbara who was the CUSO representative. He tried to kill her every time she appeared at the house. My thanks to her for persisting with our friendship.

A House in Zambia

The people of 250 Zambezi Road – the Simons

Jack and Ray lived in the main house, I lived in the medium sized house nearest to the gate (built and owned by the Simons' son, Johan), and a South African woman called Cecilia Masondo lived in the back cottage. In later years, I was to form very important friendships with the wider Simons and Masondo families. A young South African man called Sam Nkwe lived with Jack and Ray, whose own children, by now young adults, were in South Africa.

Comrade Jack and Comrade Ray, as they were universally known, were key people in the South African Communist Party which had an important historical relationship and inter-twining with the ANC.[10] Although they were both elderly, I could see that they worked very hard and seemed to have lots of visitors and meetings. As I came to learn, most of their visitors were other ANC or SACP people, and others were lecturers and researchers from the University of Zambia. The visitors came to work, for friendship, for edible food (always fresh and simple, often home-grown, and always offered with kindness and generosity) and for intellectual food.

There was no shortage of these things: Ray had been an active union organiser and women's equality fighter since her early teenage-hood in Latvia before she went to South Africa.[11] Once there, she continued her organising activities, founded the famous Food and Canning Workers' Union, and for a while was an MP. Jack had been an academic and teacher – firstly as Professor at the University of Cape Town, then, when they had to leave South Africa in the 1960s because of their political activities, he

---

10 Jack and Ray are outstanding public figures in South Africa – where they are seen as heroes, and I think it is still too early to really judge their public stature which may increase over time. If you go on the internet, you will find many, many references to them (Ray also used her maiden name, Alexander), to their lives, their publications, and their contributions to the South African struggle. A good interview with them, a biography of Ray, and a tribute to both can be found at
http://www.sacp.org.za/main.php?include=docs/biography/2006/rjsimon.html
http://www.sacp.org.za/main.php?include=docs/biography/2006/ray.html
http://www.sacp.org.za/main.php?include=docs/biography/2006/tribute.html
I cannot possibly do justice to their public personae in this piece, that is best left to their biographers and the historians. All I can attempt is to write about them as the remarkable people I had the good fortune to live near, their friendship, and their huge impact on me as a young person trying to understand Southern Africa.

11 Her autobiography was published in November 2004: Ray Alexander Simons, *All my life and all my strength*, edited by Raymond Suttner, STE publishers, Johannesburg, 2004.

went to teach at Manchester University for a while, which is also where they both worked to complete their seminal publication *Class and Colour in South Africa, 1850-1950*. Then he was Professor of Sociology at UNZA, before 'retiring' to become a teacher to the young South African guerrillas in the camps of Angola and elsewhere and the Chairman of the then ANC's Constitutional Committee, which was the pre-cursor of the committee which drew up today's South African Constitution. I think that Jack's study, the outside of which is now painted a hideous green, is where the South African Constitution began its formal incubation.

Slowly, organically, I began to realize who I was living with. A lot of my observations and therefore understanding about this came about because, as I was in the house nearest to the entrance gates, it fell to me and Bobby to open and close them for visitors. One of the most frequent visitors I would open the gates to was Thabo Mbeki. The other way I grew to understand what an exceptionally interesting place I was living in came as Jack and Ray invited me to join Sam and themselves, and whichever other friends were with them (often Hugh Macmillan), on their daily evening stroll around the nearby shanty compound called N'gombe[12] Compound.

The walk was the best part of my day when I was in Lusaka. For about an hour, the last hour of light, we would walk and talk all around N'gombe. We would talk between ourselves but we would also enjoy frequent conversations with the N'gombe residents we met on our way – most of whom knew Jack and Ray, and all of whom knew of them. Jack and Ray were particularly interested in how people built their homes and gardened their plots and arranged their lives – in Zambia you call this 'how people are staying'. So we were normally invited in for discussion and to see how people were extending their homes wall by wall, as income allowed, how their vegetables were doing and any problems encountered (Ray often had good advice to offer here, it seemed to me her vegetable advice was based on more practical experience than Jack's), we discussed the prices of basic commodities, transport problems, births and deaths, peoples' health matters, and of course, politics. Towards the end of the walk, as we were headed home back to the suburbs, Jack would generally sum up our findings and locate them in his encyclopaedic mental map of 'how people stay'.

---

12 Which means cow in Cinyanja.

The point of importance is that they, we, were quite genuinely fascinated by the minutiae of peoples' lives – it was understood between us that the granularity of how people stay formed the basis for any bigger view of the world and, most centrally, of political understanding. We thrived on our daily detail update, and it was good for all of us to have some exercise too.

Ray's influence on me was different. While she generally deferred to Jack on analytical matters, she lived her politics by helping people to organise themselves (politically and in their personal lives). I once employed a house watchman, Laban, who couldn't read. Ray set about teaching him literacy and gave him communist documents with which to practice. This meant that he read aloud all night near my window – droning on about the dialectic and stalwarts and one for all. It was unbearable.

She also encouraged people to live life to the full, and was always taking care of people. She was always there if I got ill, and when I was pregnant, although I was always well, she was motherly and supportive – just what I needed. Throughout my time there, I was always mindful of how much Jack and Ray missed their own children in South Africa. As they used to say, everyone in exile was painfully separated from family and friends.

I realised that both Ray and Cecilia played motherly roles towards the younger ANC comrades in Lusaka, in addition to their professional duties. For the young women in exile, it seemed that they were going to be locked out of their country and normal life for the indefinite future – in the early to mid-1980s, apartheid was becoming an increasingly repressive system. So they all had to ask the question, 'how will I ever have children?'. Ray advised people to have children anyway, while you still could, single or not. Cecilia (more on her below) was of a more traditional school, and counselled people not to have children until they were in better circumstances – not while they were living as refugees with an uncertain future. This contradictory advice coming from two powerful women in the same compound was noted and discussed by all bystanders. The upshot was that many comrades decided not to wait for their children, and the ANC set up a crèche/pre-school in Lusaka – Oxfam was one of the first donors in 1983-84 (see chapter 4).

As a young person and as a foreigner living in Zambia, living with Jack and Ray was the best entrée I could possibly ever have had not only to my Zambian neighbourhood but also to the world as seen through a Marxian structural lens, a very human one. It was unusual for a *mzungu* (white person) to be walking around the shanty compounds in those days; now, with the high-walled fortress mentality of Lusaka, I doubt it would be possible at all.

Jack and Ray both returned to South Africa as quickly as they could after the process towards democracy was begun; they did not even wait for the indemnities which were being arranged for returning exiles. Oxfam bought the property from them, after a painful quarrel about the final price, and moved the office to the compound (see chapter 11).

Jack and Ray were delighted that they could move home - they wanted to be with their family, to get on with their work inside the country, and, as they were both getting on in years, to die there. They settled back into a flat in Cape Town, in Vredehoek. Jack died in July 1995, and Ray in September 2004.

Sam Nkwe

Sam Nkwe[13] was a gentle, learned, humorous guy, who was billeted with the Simons – they were very close together. I think he worked in the International Department in the ANC, and was a political instructor at Mazimbu – an ANC base in Tanzania. He was also one of Jack's star pupils on the political courses he ran in Angola.[14] He was a dear friend to us all. Sam and I considered ourselves to be the 'youth' on the compound and this gave us some licence to privately discuss, always with affection, the ways of the older generation.

As I began to meet more ANC exiles socially, I also learned that one had to adopt a certain way of conversation. You could not make ordinary small talk – you couldn't directly ask people what they did, where they had just come from, where they were going, what their real name was (a lot of exiles 'sailed under different colours' as Jack put it), and so on – because that information might be deemed sensitive. So you had to talk very much

---

13 Sam Nkwe was his *nom de guerre*. His real name was Wolpe Sapnath Poho. He was born at Bethanie, Rustenburg on 20 December 1952, the second of six sons of Othilia and Godfrey Poho. He died on 6 May 1984 at Mazimbu in Tanzania. His obituary was written by Jack and Ray in *The African Commuist*, 99, 4th Quarter, 1984,111-12.

14 See the book *Comrade Jack* for a full account of Jack's life as a teacher in the ANC Angola camps in the 1970s: *Comrade Jack. The political lectures and diary of Jack Simons, Novo Catengue*, edited by Marion Sparg, Jenny Schreiner and Gwen Ansell, Johannesburg, STE publishers, 2001.

in the present, and hold fast onto any common reference point you could find. The usual one, the most common bond, was that we were all away from our families, in a foreign land. I sometimes used to think that Zambia and 'how people stayed' seemed as different to the South Africans, whether black or white, as it did to me.

Sam died young and unnecessarily – he was an asthmatic (as was Jack). While he was living with Jack and Ray in Lusaka, there were quite a few occasions when Jack would rush him to hospital in the early hours in their old Renault 4. Sam had an asthma attack while he was staying at Mazimbu, where they were not able to treat him, and died there in May 1984.

Cecilia Masondo

Cecilia Masondo - I have to say last but by no means least – lived in the back cottage and was a very important friend to me and also a woman of great standing in the ANC.[15] Soon after I moved into my house, I was standing on a chair scrubbing the kitchen walls, when Cecilia appeared and said 'Ah! That's what I like to see, a white woman doing good housework!'. That was how we met. She had come to greet her new neighbour and I was lucky to have won approval in an area of life Cecilia considered very important – working hard to keep oneself and one's house clean.

Cecilia worked hard on all fronts – as PA to Oliver Tambo, the President of the ANC whilst Mandela was in jail, as a motherly figure to many young comrades, and in keeping her own cottage spotless. Even though she was disabled, having lost a leg in a train accident many years earlier, she worked harder than most people and had very little time for lazy and unprincipled people – her standards were very exacting. People had a natural respect for her.

But she did get tired and that was the one thing I could sometimes help with – I could sit her down, get her a drink, maybe make something to eat, play some music, and we would chat about our day. Often I could give her a lift into work as she was perpetually infuriated by the ANC transport logistics. Although walking was uncomfortable for her, she would always insist on being dropped off a couple of blocks away from her office, 'for security reasons'.

---

15 Again, I can only write about Cecilia as my friend and not about her role in the ANC and the South African struggle. I think this latter job has yet to be done.

Cecilia thought about her family all the time, and missed them sorely. Some of them were able to visit her, and although she was proud of what all her children were doing in the various countries where they lived, she was made for running a home for an extended family and I think she so wished she could have been doing that.

Shortly after I left Zambia, something terrible happened to her family. Her son Vusi had married a young Zimbabwean woman and they had two young daughters in Harare. Vusi was an ANC guerrilla, travelling around all the time – he is now in the South African army. A parcel bomb in the shape of a TV was sent to their home to target him. Unfortunately, it was his wife who turned it on, and was instantly killed. The two daughters – Phumie (5 years) and Lungi (6 months) – were in the flat at the time. Cecilia went immediately to Harare to take charge of the daughters and bring them up with her in Lusaka (not in Zambezi Road, she had moved by then). They lived happily with her for 4 years, until her own health started to fail and so she brought them to live with her daughter, also called Phumie, in London. Shortly afterwards, in the early 1990s, Cecilia died peacefully in her sleep in Lusaka. She had not managed to return to South Africa, but was given a hero's funeral in Johannesburg.

250 Zambezi Road – the place

At that time, the perimeter fence of the property was just link wire with lots of bougainvillea decorating it and a solid line of giant aloes protecting it. When someone came to the gate, you could see who they were and you could see who was passing on the street. Today, the high walls surrounding every property seem to have changed the nature of the neighbourhood.

Apart from their work, Comrades Jack and Ray were very interested in their property and land – they took a lot of trouble as landlords to me for example. More importantly, they were always aware that they were fortunate to own a home in Lusaka, when so many of their comrades didn't. So they were generous in using their home and land for others, and they originally built the back cottage (Cecilia's home) for Oliver Tambo to use when he was in Zambia before the ANC established its exile HQ there.

They were very interested in the planting and care of the trees on the property, watering, digging the circle of earth around the base of the tree so that it could be properly manured and retain moisture. They were very against all chemicals, and very keen on growing trees from which we could eat - we had avocados for nine months of the year,[16] limes, lemons, oranges, paw paws, bananas, guavas, lychees, peaches, and vegetables. They didn't do flowerbeds, but all available native species of flowers which didn't need irrigating flourished. Most importantly, they grew protea trees, and the drive was lined with poinsettia trees which I think have now gone. We often toured the plot together discussing all the tree developments.

Cecilia was also interested in the garden, there were lots of banana palms by her house and she also grew vegetables. She was particularly fond of asparagus, and had a patch of it just by her cottage (asparagus is a long term project, it takes some years to mature). Now and again, I would notice that some extremely athletic-looking young men would be hanging around in our compound. I slowly came to know that these were ANC guerrillas (I think they used to sling their arms behind a bush), who had been detailed to guard us when there was a security alert. These blokes didn't have anything to do except guard us. As I have mentioned, Cecilia could not abide idleness, so she set them to work slashing [17] the grass and keeping the place in order while they were there. You could see from the body language that they didn't like this, but nobody would countermand Cecilia, so they buckled down. On one such day there came a terrible shriek from her end of the compound – one of the MKs[18] had slashed her asparagus patch. Idleness compounded with carelessness – he was in big trouble.

When I last saw the plot in October 2004, I was really pleased to see that although the buildings on the plot are rather neglected, the trees which Jack and Ray planted and reared are all healthy and glossy – it made me realise they are more of a lasting legacy.

One day, Mr Banda, the young man Jack and Ray employed in the house

---

16 John Clark, onetime Oxfam campaigner, later with the World Bank, recalled (15 October 2007) 'Yes - I do remember Zambezi Road clearly, and being awed by the chance to meet and get to know Jack and Ray. My recollection of them was that within minutes of meeting them you knew they were far from ordinary! They just exuded passion, commitment and creativity, didn't they! My other lasting memory was of the wonderful avocados that were just dropping from that big tree in the yard. At that time you had to be relatively well-to-do to afford avocados in UK - so a real treat!'

17 'Slashing' in this part of Africa is the verb meaning to cut grass, using a sort of flat-bladed long knife. It provides casual labour for countless people, but I noticed that a lawnmower is used now in our compound. Also the gardener now waters the grass which Jack and Ray would never have allowed, water being scarce.

18 Members of Umkhonto we Sizwe, the ANC's armed wing, were known as MKs.

and garden did a terrible thing. While we were all out, he stripped all the avocado trees of their fruit (most of it very unripe), and set up shop outside the gate to sell his many basket loads of rock-hard, undersized pears. Nobody wanted to buy of course, so by the time we got home his failed income-generation plan plus the damage to our crop was all too evident. This was a very big matter in our compound – not only was a whole year's crop wasted (we all loved eating them, especially the fruit from the tall tree by the side of my house) but also a very big justice question was raised, what was the right thing to do with him? Needless to say, Jack, Ray and Cecilia focussed primarily on the justice question. I think he kept his job but had to undergo a lot of re-education.

Ric Goodman (the Oxfam Representative in Zambia in 2004) feels that the Zambezi Road plot is really the ancestral home of Oxfam in Zambia – I do hope it makes sense for Oxfam to move back there,[19] and I hope this and others' contributions will give us our history back.

Susie in Zambian village, 1982

---

19 At various times in the recent past, Oxfam has attempted to move out of or sell 250 Zambezi Road. Fortunately, saner counsels have prevailed and that notion has been dropped.

A House in Zambia

Susie with Zambian family, 1982

Susie Smith in Zambian youth project, 1982

Susie with Zambian child, 1982

7. ANNE LLOYD-WILLIAMS (interim, mid-1984)[1]

Susie Smith gave me a superb handover in mid-1984, well-organised and in just the right detail so that I felt fully equipped but not overwhelmed. The handover included instructions on caring for Bobby, the dog. Susie demonstrated one of his party tricks which she told me he did without being taught. When his brush was produced, he went into the kitchen, nudged out a chair, and stood with front paws up on the seat so that his large black back was offered at just the right angle.

One of my strongest memories of 250 Zambezi Road is waking in the night to the sweet smell of 'Queen of the Night' wafting in from the window, and the chinking from Bobby's collar as he moved slightly on the balcony outside, on close guard at all times.

The compound in Zambezi Road was a good base for a job involving lots of travel. In those days an Oxfam Field Director would be on the road for at least two-thirds of the time. While I was away, Jack and Ray Simons kept an eye on things and fed Bobby. He had to be put on a diet each time I returned.

The Simons were immensely kind to me. I was invited many times for a meal, including Ray's special, a guava crumble that challenged the teeth. Jack and Ray would take an evening walk around the neighbourhood and I sometimes went with them. They seemed genuinely interested in my impressions of Zambia. I had a measure of how they valued each and every person no matter how callow! I longed to ask about their lives and especially Ray's childhood in Lithuania, but felt this might be intrusive.

How strange to return to Zambezi Road in 2002 and find their house turned into the Oxfam office. As I think on their personal qualities I realise Susie also came to share them.

I hope their welcoming, listening, strong and optimistic spirit will live on in those working there now.

---

1 Anne worked as interim Field Director for three months in mid-1984, taking over from Susie Smith, who was six months' pregnant with Sarah, before handing over to Mike Edwards.

A House in Zambia

Anne Lloyd-Williams, 1987

8. MIKE EDWARDS (1984 – 88)

I can add little to Susie's wonderfully evocative description of 250 Zambezi Road and its place in history, large and small, except for a few footnotes, so to speak.[1] I do remember it as a great place to live – part-sanctuary, part-university, part boarding-house and part-agricultural commune! Like others I suspect, I just loved the place, or more the spirit and the symbol of the place than the place itself – the conversations that took place there and the plans that were hatched; the relationships that cemented themselves and the spirits that were constantly kept aloft. I don't think I've ever been as happy and fulfilled either before or since. Why was that?

The Simons

The times, of course 'were a changing', though I don't think we knew it at the time, certainly not Jack and Ray who, as late as 1987, spoke longingly of returning to a free South Africa only as a distant possibility. From there on, it all happened so quickly. Did I realise who I was living with, and the significance of the visitors that formed a constant stream through the big front gates? Not really, though years later Thabo Mbeki (at that time aide-de camp to Oliver Tambo and a regular visitor to the compound) remembered his interactions with me and others in some speeches he gave after reading a book I wrote later called Future Positive.[2] Jack and Ray, of course, were the life and steel of the place, and a dog-eared copy of their master-work, *Class and Colour in South Africa 1850-1950*, takes pride of place on my Ford Foundation bookshelf along with the small marble eagle they gave me just before I left Lusaka in October 1988. It's a small, crudely-fashioned piece, but I like to think it carries something of the spirit of this remarkable pair, so it will never leave my desk. It's all I have of them now, and very precious. I never went back to Zambia, but my time there with Oxfam was what formed me as a person.

---

[1] This was written in November 2004. Mike's job title changed from Field Director to Regional Representative in 1986.
[2] Michael Edwards, *Future Positive: International Co-operation in the 21st Century*, London, Earthscan Publications, 2004. Thabo Mbeki wrote that '*Future Positive* captures the essence of the dilemmas of current economic relations between rich and poor countries.'

A House in Zambia

Bobby, the dog

And then of course there was Bobby, the crossbred German shepherd/border collie that went with the house, and with the job! I come from a cat family, but this guy was something else – a total character, and known near and far, especially among Canadians. As Susie says, they were especially at risk, never more so than when foolishly creeping around the wrong side of the house as though they were burglars. We almost had to put him down after a particularly nasty (or effective) attack (or defence - you decide!) on John Van Mossel's (the CUSO representative) wife, but luckily he was spared the lethal injection after I spoke up for him. I heard that Bobby died soon after I left Lusaka and he was moved to another compound and another member of Oxfam's staff – was it a broken heart, or am I just being romantic?

The Oxfam staff

Talking of Oxfam staff, what a team! The mighty Wilson Kaonza, driver extraordinaire whom I remember perched precariously astride the tiny and useless moped I sold to him before I left as he tottered at 20 miles an hour from Lusaka to his house in Chongwe; Daka, administrative assistant and general man-about-town, whose house was permanently about-to-be finished if only he could get that one final raise; Dorothy Chikula, who kept us all in check from her impregnable command post in the CUSA Building, ably assisted by Christine Chinzewe; Francis Banda, whom I stole from the Zambia Council for Social Development when the office began to expand, and Lucy Muyoyeta, who went on to achieve great things with the Soros gang [Open Society Institute] in South Africa and is now back home with ActionAid. Not forgetting the Malawi contingent of course – Tony Klouda and his family, trying to reform the primary health care system single-handedly and foment revolution in the process! I'd like to think my regular trips across the border were warranted by programme development and not just by the availability of dark stout beer, Cadbury's dairy milk, crisps and other elements of a balanced and healthy diet. I couldn't buy much in Lusaka at the time because so little was produced locally or imported because of the South African blockade – even rice and bread were scarce, so I made my own (at least the bread). The dreaded TanZam railway also led to one of the worst, and funniest, phone conversations I've ever had:

'do you want the good news or the bad news?' the freight company said down the line. 'I'll have the good news please', I said. 'OK then, you've still got four books and a hockey stick.' The rest – all my worldly goods from photos to tapes to clothes to my TV – were stolen from a railway siding in Dar es Salaam a few months after I arrived. Someone there is still watching my scratchy videotape of the 1981 FA Cup Final, and I want it back!

Malawi

I remember Malawi as a bizarre place that required a segmented personality to survive, especially when sitting next to Cecilia Kadzamira, Kamuzu Banda's 'Official Hostess' (no, not the trolley or the kind you get at the coffee-house). Oxfam supported what few NGOs existed in Malawi at the time, and she seemed to be Patron of all of them, so a seat next to her was guaranteed for the visiting Oxfam Field Director. Did she personally arrange the 'car crashes' that wiped out so much of the Malawian opposition? Maybe, maybe not, but she was certainly implicated. Pass the sugar please…

Rich, surreal experiences

The Oxfam job was full of such surreal experiences, which is why it was so rich. Father Benignus, the Irish Catholic priest who had built a semi-utopia among the Lozi but who still requested regular deliveries of videotapes ('The ones with as much sex and violence as you can find please') whenever I visited him to check up on the Angolan refugees in the far west; sipping huge glass bottles of Zairean beer with Robin Palmer under a starlit sky on the banks of the Luapula River, staring across from the relative safety of the Zambian side into the slowly-unfolding chaos of the other bank.[3] Best of all was the Oxfam Volunteers Tour which had a personal audience with the then President Kenneth Kaunda. Their group leader, Pauline, strode right up to him and gave him a traditional ChiChewa greeting in the broadest of broad Yorkshire vowels, 'mu-li bwan-ji Mr President,' she said, leaving KK momentarily lost for words! Then he invited them to tea. Great stuff.

---

3 Note by Robin Palmer: in my Zambia Tour Report for October / November 1987, I observed that 'Mike and I were thrashed at bar football by the entire drinking population of Kawambwa.'

A House in Zambia

Looking back, did we do any good? By today's standards much of the programming was unsophisticated, maybe, though it was sincere and heartfelt, and path-breaking in its own small ways. But it was certainly headed in the right direction, spurred on by a remarkable succession of good people in the Oxfam Office and fondly remembered by the Doctors, the Nurses and the Industrial Health Tribunal (the code-words we gave to the Liberation Movements when communicating by telex). Like all remembered times, they were probably never as good as I think they were, but if Oxfam does return to Zambezi Road,[4] it will feel as though the wheel has turned again, and come to rest for a while, in a special place, in a special part of the world, dedicated to the memory of two remarkable people, and sure in the conviction that another world is always possible.

Mike Edwards, 1982

---

4   It has since Mike wrote this piece in November 2004.

9. PUSHPANATH (1988 – 92)

What a splendid recall and what an interesting way Susie brings to life two great heroes of the South African struggle and other not so minor characters associated with them.

I, Push, solemnly declare what I am saying[1] is the truth and nothing but the truth as I remember it and I cannot live up to the herstory of Susie or for that matter that phenomenon called Dr Edwards whose past was so formidable that I used to read the fantastic field reports by Susie in hiding to take on Dr Edwards - I am moving ahead of myself here and that is another story for another time...

First impressions

My first impression of the Zambezi Road compound was of a massive area with many houses in it, many trees, almost a subtropical forest, and massive houses spread across the compound following the logic of the owners which always baffled me. I remember the first week I was brought to Zambezi Road straight from the airport and given one of the rooms. The first thing I noticed was the house was very poorly maintained and it had lots of funny English cutleries, pots and pans, looking like they were very Victorian and I wondered what will I do with them. Of course Uma, my wife, would not touch them because she suspected that most of them were used to cook meat and she even started to cook outside with three stones and firewood until she felt that every last bit of grease (she was convinced it was all animal fat) was removed from the stoves.

In one of those generous moments of a newly arrived, I was given the responsibility of Bobby, the human dog. I accepted it most gracefully - I think, wanting to demonstrate what an open minded Indian I am and not wanting to hurt the English sensibilities towards animals and also because I knew that people visiting from the UK always enquired after Bobby first and so I was aware that my reputation was at stake a bit, and I needed to be careful and all that. I was simply stumped when suddenly Ray Simons arrived from the smarter of the houses and said I had to provide 'bones' for the dog. I was so stunned by this rather esoteric demand that I developed a

---

1   This was written in October 2004 with a postscript added after Susie's death in June 2006.

deep suspicion of the place and what it held for quite some time. But somehow we got into agreement that I would bring the bones but Ray would help to cook or do whatever one does to feed a dog. Anyway, as soon as the family arrived after a few months we felt that the house was too big for us, having lived in India for most of my life in a house 20ft x 20ft, besides we used to get lost frequently there. As if it was not enough, Ahir, our second son who was barely 18 months old, kept peeing on the wooden floor no matter what we did to get him to use the toilet. Vexed and weary, we soon took a smaller apartment and moved house. We took Bobby with us though because Uma had become very attached to him and we did not think that we had much option to renegotiate the ownership with Ray, having realised what a formidable person she was by that time.

I did not have such good fortune to spend such wonderful time with Jack and Ray, as much as Susie did, but I managed to get to them when we shared the food I cooked with Ray, especially when she got people around for a meal. Jack used to nod off after engaging me in a very rich dialogue on the Indian peasant struggle, but Ray would join in and we would start to talk about Zambia and she would take me on a tour of the compound and show me all the trees – I remember once counting eighty one different trees and plants. There were many evenings I spent time with them, but things changed when my family arrived. For the first time in our lives we ate avocados in plenty and ShyAm and Ahir would run around everywhere and play in that massive place – we were warned many times not to leave them outside unattended like that because the compound had many snakes and so on.

Oxfam moves into 250 Zambezi Road

But there was some invisible connection to me, Oxfam and to that house, as I soon realized. As soon as the situation was changing in South Africa, the Simons were offering the house for sale and our dear old Robin Palmer convinced all and sundry in HQ and we bought the house.

We were so relieved. For the first time all the staff were in one building and we had lots of space to park the two vehicles and we could have many partners and Oxfam advisory teams meeting in that building. We felt so free...

The house I stayed in became the meeting place, sleeping place and party place in the evening when the live band music by the then Front Line Musicians and later the Burning Youth would play for all of us.

The big tree (all hugged in a snaky embrace by flaming bougainvillea during the season) was a special place which was in the back of the building which we used as the front for the office. It is under this tree that I remember most of the meetings took place. The first Black Consciousness training was held for staff and partners; Fr Peter Henriot discussing with us advocacy capacity in Zambia; the first programme impact measurement meeting with all the Southern African representatives in Oxfam; the first boisterous strategic plan was conceived; the best parties and send-offs and many small significant and not so significant meetings and visitors, including the letter-writing campaign and all the major meetings regarding the drought in Zambia were held there along with all the mess and the muddle that we hatched. Under the same tree when I went to do the Big Noise campaign[2] training, *The Post* newspaper interviewed me this time after ten years, and the sense of déjà vu was unbearable for me.

The small house was converted into a guesthouse to the chagrin of many of our visiting staff and I lived there for six months during my extension when Lucy as the Regional Representative occupied the main house and Lucy managed me at that time. And we shared so much about Zambia, our work, and our lives with a bottle or two of Mozi (the local bottled beer).

Even though we had a proper walled compound built by then, we used to keep the gates open so our partners from the villages could come into the Oxfam office openly and freely. We did our best to reciprocate the warmth and hospitality that we were offered by our partners when we went to visit them.

This property by virtue of all these endearing and enduring memories had become a part of the myth and legend of Oxfam and I did not realise then an important part of me too.

In 2003, when Mahesh (the Oxfam Country Representative in the late 1990s) told me that Oxfam was selling the property and moving into a

---

2 The Big Noise campaign involved a global petition calling for an end to the unfair rules of world trade; 17,800,000 people signed the petition presented to the WTO ministerial meeting in Hong Kong in December, 2005.

A House in Zambia

rented place I could not bear it; there were tears in my eyes. I just thought what a sentimental old fool I have become.

A kind of postscript

A few lines to remember Susie: she has left us, but her memories and the things she stood for remain in many splendored ways.

For starters, we are back in 250 Zambezi Road – the office is in full flow. I am sure she is keeping a close and friendly watch on the happenings there and having a few chuckles to herself.

Pushpanath, 1990

Pushpanath & Bobby the famous dog, 1990

10. LUCY MUYOYETA (1993-97)

Joining Oxfam

In writing about 250 Zambezi Road,[1] I must start from the beginning. The beginning for me was joining Oxfam as a Field Officer in 1985. At the time, the Oxfam office was situated in downtown Lusaka the capital city of Zambia; 2nd Floor CUSA House, Cairo Road to be specific. It was then I was introduced to 250 Zambezi Road and its famous inhabitants, Ray and Jack Simons. It took me a while though to realise just how famous these two were. But even when I did get to know who they really were, sadly my interaction with them was rather limited. For the most part I interacted with them when I just happened to be in the car with Dorothy Chikula the Oxfam Administrator who was going to sort out maintenance related works. Bobby the famous dog (the reasons for which he gained his fame still elude me) was the other rather permanent inhabitant of 250 Zambezi Road. He survived Susie Smith (RIP), was passed on to Mike Edwards and then on to K. Pushpanath. I joined Oxfam when Mike Edwards was the Oxfam Country Representative. I was to join all the three aforementioned by finally becoming an inhabitant of 250 Zambezi Road (from henceforth I will refer to it simply as 250). Although I never worked directly with Susie as she had left Zambia by the time I joined Oxfam, I subsequently got to know her very well.

Moving into 250 Zambezi Road

But I moved into 250 at a very different period because Ray and Jack Simons had by that time left Zambia and gone back home to South Africa. Bobby too was no longer in the compound. When Pushpanath and his family moved out and I moved in, I insisted that Bobby move with them. No amount of arm twisting or sweet talk could persuade me to keep him. Nothing against Bobby personally but, try as I might, I have failed to develop a liking for animals particularly pets. To date I do not keep any.

---

1   This was written in January 2007 and revised in September 2007. Lucy began in 1993 as Regional Representative for Zambia and Malawi, like Push, Mike and Susie before her. But in 1995 the Malawi programme went its own way, and so Lucy was 'relegated' to being Country Representative for Zambia alone.

A House in Zambia

I moved into 250 when Oxfam bought the compound in 1990 and the office shifted from downtown into the house in the compound that Ray and Jack had occupied. We did not know it then, but we were amongst the pioneers of the decamping of offices from the city into the suburbs. Today, very few respectable organisations want to work in the city as services there have deteriorated and traffic congestion has become the order of the day.

I was initially a very reluctant inhabitant of 250 because, like all my colleagues, the thought of living next to the office frightened me. But after some 'arm twisting' from Push and Francis Banda (RIP), I was persuaded. A lot can be said about these two guys in terms of their powers of persuasion especially their 'gift of the gab'. But for now I shalln't go into the details of that, suffice it to say that for a while Francis 'bouncing' Banda, Pushpanath and I were to become an inseparable threesome, brought close together by the fact that for a long while we were the only three doing programme work. Francis nicknamed 'bounce' by Push did actually bounce when he walked, this despite his poor eating habits and attendant lanky frame; don't know where the guy got the energy from.

So, I was to set up home next to the office and it generally worked well, once I reconciled myself to the fact that I no longer had a life that was private and distinct from the office's one. Not surprisingly, the entire office somehow always knew what went on in my home, who visited me, who was sneaked into my house late at night etc. Indeed especially in the early days, there were moments of serious tension between the office and my large, exuberant extended family. Those who know them know that nothing will stop them coming to visit when they want or for that matter having a party. Over time, some office colleagues became part of this extended family, and to date still enjoy good relations with my biological family. After a while, I stopped agonising over this set up, made the best of it, and enjoyed it.

At 250, we maintained an open door policy; we did not have any security people during the daytime, the gate was kept open and only closed in the evenings after working hours. I must admit this owed more to Push's more extroverted character and style, because left on my own I tend to be introverted. But, I learnt a lot from this and even after Push left and I became Country Representative in 1993 until I left in October 1997, the open door policy was maintained. Through those doors many, many people came, and whilst it is impossible to mention or even list them all, a few

Lucy Muyoyeta

have left indelible memories and I remember some of them and not in any order of importance.

Some unforgettable characters

Who can forget 'Chief' Wilson Kaonza? That man of many talents but known primarily as the Chief Pilot or Driver. Amongst his talents included great story telling, farming, and outspokenness. But what I remember most about him is the fact that here was a simple man from a very simple background who never stepped foot in school, but yet was able to hold his own as he took the many Oxfam visitors around the country. On a rather sad note, the one thing he wanted more than anything was to educate his children especially his beloved first daughter, Kelesia. But, I saw the despondency grow on his face as he narrated his children's lack of interest in school and he was particularly heartbroken when Kelesia opted to leave school and get married at a very young age.

Then there was Michael Kumwenda (RIP) and the Burning Youth. They breezed into our lives and 250 became like a second home for them. Their use of the guest house for their musical practice drove some of the staff crazy; eventually they moved on. They were to remain Zambia's top band for a while and made those of us who had associated with them when they were still fledgling youngsters very proud. In fact, a good number of us from the office and my extended family became 'groupies' and went almost everywhere the band played. Michael Kumwenda was a great showman but sadly he died too soon, and although his colleagues tried hard to keep going, it all became too difficult when Danny (one of the guitarists and like Michael very charismatic) died, followed soon after by Fred (the key-board player, with the reputation of being amongst the best in Zambia). The group still carries on today anchored by the two brothers Allan and Jack, but things are no longer the same. The Burning Youth were part of an Oxfam musical campaign against the apartheid regime in South Africa and its atrocities against the Frontline States. It involved many other musicians, but the Burning Youth stood out and as part of this campaign conducted concerts in the UK, to very positive reviews. But the story of the Burning Youth in particular and the campaign in general deserves a book of its own; there is a good story to be told.

Then there was Nawina Hamaundu (RIP) who joined us as a Projects Officer and we did not know what hit us thereafter. Totally without any inhibition, she loved to shock and while I personally found it difficult to work with her (and I asked her to leave), we became and remained good personal friends till her sudden shocking death. Even after she left Oxfam, she remained a frequent visitor to 250 and often came to tell me outrageously funny stories about what she was up to. I will always remember when Chris Dammers came to carry out the evaluation of the Eastern Province Drought Programme, the performance that Nawina gave as she told story after story that had everyone in tears from laughter, though I seem to recall Chris did not find them so funny, because after all poor guy had a job to do and there he was being told stories about the 'darker' side of the drought programme. When I later visited Oxford, Chris and his wife Dianna Melrose invited me to their home and in a more relaxed atmosphere, Chris was able to really laugh about Nawina. In his description of her to Dianna, he described her as 'larger than life in all senses of the word'. Nawina was very big body wise and she did not care for dieting or gyms. As she dug into the fatty bit of the pork chops (one of her favourite foods), you could almost wipe the glee off her face.

That drought programme brought in its fair share of characters; amongst the most memorable of these was Victor Pelekamoyo. An accountant by profession and on the surface very much 'guy about town' in his very smart suits, Victor was to surprise all of us by his ability to go beyond the figures. He wasn't your typical accountant because he wrote fantastic reports (most accountants can't write); his ability to relate to people was amazing. It was a marvel to watch him training ordinary villagers accounting in Nyanja (the local language of the Eastern Province). Victor's subsequent move to Zimbabwe and Oxford is a real loss to Zambia as a whole.

I believe the story of 250 cannot be told without mention of Malitino Daka. The longest serving member of staff of Oxfam at the time I was leaving, he too was a legend. Another self taught man with very little formal education, Daka's commitment and selflessness was astounding. Starting work as a humble messenger/cleaner, he rose through the ranks to become an Administrative Assistant. Yet his commitment and humility remained intact. It was not uncommon to find, even when it was no longer his job, Daka cleaning and dusting because someone else had neglected to. He would do so with not a complaint and always smiling. But, the one 'bone of contention' between Daka and me was the filing system or shall I say the lack of it. Daka had done the filing for so long and had developed a system which resided only in his head and only he knew and understood. It therefore was virtually impossible to find documents when he was not available. I subsequently brought in someone to re-organise the entire filing system into something we could all understand.

But putting individuals and personalities aside, I think it is important to remember that 250 was the anchor of the work of Oxfam in Zambia and Malawi until Malawi got its 'independence' in 1995. Looking back now, with the knowledge that one has gained since then, it is easy to see the mistakes we made such as overextending ourselves. But one thing is for sure, we worked with total commitment and passion and it showed. There was the remarkable 23,000 letters we generated and took to the IMF/WB meetings as part of the debt cancellation campaign; the mobilisation of communities and people during the 1992/3 drought was immense; the work with grassroots communities in the Copperbelt when it was difficult to carry policy advocacy work etc.

This account is but a snapshot of one person's recollections of 250 Zambezi Road. It was a fantastic place to work and live in. I left in 1997 for a short stint with Oxfam in West Africa. In May 1998 I finally left Oxfam, but the times with Oxfam from 1985 when I joined and particularly during the time at 250 remain the best of my years professionally and personally and I have everlasting fond memories.

A House in Zambia

Lucy Muyoyeta, 1996

PART THREE:

THE OXFAM DESK OFFICER AND REGIONAL MANAGER

11. ROBIN PALMER (1987-95)

Introduction

In June 2005 I sat down to write a few words to add to the recollections begun by Susie Smith and then added to by Mike Edwards and Pushpanath. I did so in the highly appropriate setting of the Oxfam office in South Africa, in Johannesburg. I had just had a meeting with members of the South African Communist Party. So the echoes of the Simons and Zambezi Road were very strong. As many in this collection have suggested, even the possibility of such a meeting in such a place would have seemed inconceivable in the late 1980s.

The Southern Africa Desk

I worked for Oxfam for twenty years. I had the exceptional good fortune to spend the first eight of these on the Southern Africa Desk, directly linked to Oxfam's programme in Zambia. The Desk was a really exciting place to be. The liberation of Southern Africa was reaching a climax, though few of us would have predicted that at the time. Oxfam was running a Frontline Africa campaign, in which Susie Smith played a prominent role. Zambia and Zimbabwe were key frontline states. We had a huge emergency programme in Mozambique. The Desk had two charismatic leaders in first Peter Wiles and then the late Odhiambo Anacleti. Both were passionately committed to the liberation of Southern Africa. On Zambia, I worked with the endlessly resourceful Izzy Birch, Desk Administrator, and the highly supportive Claire Humphreys, Desk Assistant. Within Oxfam, relations between desks and country offices could sometimes become strained. I think I can reasonably claim that in the case of Zambia they were overwhelming positive and mutually supportive. Izzy, Claire and I had enormous respect for the Zambia programme and for the people who ran it – the 'Zammers' as Izzy nicknamed them (to distinguish them from the 'Zimmers' of Zimbabwe!). Many of the Lusaka staff visited Oxford from time to time, and the three of us all visited Zambia. So I worked directly with three of the Representatives, Mike Edwards, Pushpanath and Lucy Muyoyeta, whose memoirs appear in this collection, and, in Oxford, with Susie on her

A House in Zambia

Front Line Africa book.¹ We all worked hard, but we also had a lot of fun together – which is really important in development work, as in life.

Indeed, my eight-year working relationship with the Oxfam office in Lusaka proved to be one of the outstanding joys of my Oxfam career. Every time I went to Zambia, it felt like coming home. This was doubtless because I had worked in Lusaka for six years in the 1970s as a history lecturer at the University of Zambia. That was without question the most exciting and productive time of my academic life. Out of a seminar which I ran emerged the moderately famous book I edited with Neil Parsons, *The Roots of Rural Poverty in Central and Southern Africa* (Heinemann, 1977). The book sought to offer an historical perspective to debates on rural development, arguing that the nature of the inherited colonial economies of Southern Africa 'cannot be understood, and therefore be changed wittingly, without historical analysis of how and why contemporary social and economic distortions originated.' (p.5). I was particularly pleased when a number of the reviewers commented on the fact that the majority of contributors were based at UNZA. A much loved, indeed revered, colleague at the university was the Professor of Sociology, Jack Simons.

250 Zambezi Road

I joined Oxfam in 1987, in the newly created post of Desk Officer for Zambia, Zimbabwe and the SADC Region. I did that job for four years and then, in 1991, I became Regional Manager for Zambia, Malawi, Angola and Mozambique, a job that also lasted for four years. So I visited 250 Zambezi Road on many occasions. Indeed, within a week of joining, I was whisked off to Lusaka, then on to Victoria Falls for a Southern Africa regional meeting, at which I was introduced to the famous 'Doctors' (ANC), 'Nurses' (SWAPO) and 'IHT' (COSATU). I was fortunate enough to travel extensively throughout Zambia with Oxfam, including places I had never been to when I was at UNZA, such as the north-west (with Lucy) and Luapula and the north (with Mike).

Of all the Oxfam offices I visited in my twenty-year career with Oxfam, 250 Zambezi Road in its 'struggle' days stands out as the one which had

---

1   Susanna Smith, *Front Line Africa – The Right to a Future* (Oxford, Oxfam, 1990). I contributed the section on land reform in Zimbabwe, 1980-90.

most resonance for me. It was a really great working environment, as this collection amply illustrates. It was excellent for meetings with partners, for doing interviews, for team meetings, for having parties, and for much else. And having all those ANC connections certainly added to its appeal, as least for me. I've described in chapter 12 how I came to buy the compound for Oxfam when Jack and Ray Simons were finally able to return home to South Africa in 1990.

When I became a Regional Manager it was very clear to me that Zambia/Malawi [2] was the jewel in the crown of Oxfam's Southern Africa programmes: in fact it could hold its head against any Oxfam programme anywhere.

Once Oxfam moved from Cairo Road in the centre of town into the compound on 250 Zambezi Road in Roma suburb, we[3] operated a deliberate 'open door' policy for partners. We reckoned that if any partner had made the effort to trek out there – it was not far from the University of Zambia, where I'd lived in the 1970s – then we had the responsibility to listen to them. The redoubtable Malitino Daka built up a very useful Resource Centre and made it available to partners and Oxfam sent people from other parts of Southern Africa to Lusaka to look at the model he had established. There was an annual meeting which was a genuine attempt on Oxfam's part to listen to its partners.

The Oxfam Lusaka team

We produced Country Representatives – Susie, Mike, Push, Lucy – like the Welsh used to produce rugby fly halves, just amazingly talented people, who served their full terms and brought their own special qualities to the place and the programme. They had the wisdom and maturity to respect what their predecessors had done and to build on it. We shall not see their like again.

So there was great leadership and, equally important, there were also strong and highly committed support staff. Intelligent and sensitive

---

2   Oxfam ran a joint programme in Zambia and Malawi until 1995 when an office was re-opened in Blantyre. Prior to that there had been a highly innovative pilot programme in Mulanje, run by two formidable women, Colettah Chitsike and the late Stella Chirwa, which subtly sought to promote democratic ways of doing things in local government during Banda's dictatorship.

3   Even though I have now left Oxfam, I use the 'we' throughout partly for sentimental reasons but also for grammatical ease.

management allowed everyone to feel valued and able to make a contribution – as I regularly saw for myself when attending team meetings. So no one felt excluded. This in turn resulted in great continuity and the retention of institutional memory, a critical factor. So there emerged a genuine sense of belonging to a real team and the incredible motivation that came with that.

One outstanding team member was the vastly experienced Wilson Kaonza, a driver who seemed to know every metre of a huge country and, because he travelled to the programme so much, also knew a very great deal about what was really going on behind the facade of 'official business' with the partners. He could recognise a bullshitter when he met one, often long before a Project Officer did! I found Wilson to be a person of great resourcefulness and much wisdom and kindness, a wonderful travelling companion. In later years, Oxfam sought to do away with drivers, which was a mistake at many levels, including a lack of recognition of just how much knowledge they had in their heads.

For a time, Oxfam Zambia operated an excellent induction process whereby potential programme staff were taken on tour with established staff to see how they interacted with communities. In such a way, we recruited the late Francis Banda, who lacked the education qualifications which Oxfam normally sought in a programme officer, but who more than made up for it in all manner of other ways.

Oxfam Zambia were also pioneers in Oxfam's campaigning work on debt and structural adjustment. Zambia was in some senses a laboratory guinea pig for the IMF, as Kevin Watkins notes in chapter 22, and Oxfam sought to publicise and expose the impact that its policies were having on the poor.[4]

Responding to the 1992/3 drought

Arguably, Oxfam Zambia's finest hour was the magnificent team response to the 1992/3 drought, the worst the country (and the region) had suffered to that point. It was just amazing what they all achieved then, way,

---

4 This began with: John Clark with Caroline Allison, *Zambia – Debt and Poverty* (Oxford, Oxfam, 1989). I was somewhat disillusioned to discover subsequently that Florence Tembo, a Lusaka widow about whom John Clark, head of Oxfam's modest Campaigns team, had written so movingly, was not in fact a real person but a composite created for purposes of constructing an argument.

and way beyond the call of duty. [5] A special mention of Francis Banda, who died in 2005, seems appropriate here – 'Bouncing Banda', as Push dubbed him, really came into his own at that time. Push's experience in India was also critically important; not just for Oxfam's response, but for that of the country as a whole. His contribution was immense, both in terms of leadership and by insisting that Oxfam's approach be based on what some considered two heroic assumptions:
1. it is possible to approach relief within the framework of development;
2. it is feasible to facilitate, motivate, mobilise, and train local people to take charge of the relief effort.

In 1992/3 Push and the Zambia team proved that this was indeed possible. As he later wrote:

> *The approach adopted by Oxfam in Zambia aimed not only to empower the immediate constituency — the people affected by the drought — but also those who worked alongside them, and ultimately the donors themselves, who became involved in the struggles of ordinary people in an active and dynamic way.*[6]

A regional centre?

In 1995, just before my post was restructured and Oxfam began its curious process of regionalisation, I discussed with Lucy whether Lusaka might become Oxfam's regional management centre for Southern Africa, as it had by far the most experienced support staff in the region. Characteristically, Lucy had the honesty to decline, saying that the Lusaka

---

[5] In my Zambia tour report for November 1992 I wrote: 'Extraordinary things have happened in the Eastern Province this year. Parts of the province (especially in the Luangwa Valley) have been hard hit by the drought, the worst since 1949. It has to be said that the amazing example set by Oxfam staff, working all hours of the day and night and never accepting 'no' or 'it's impossible' for answers must have made a deep impression. It would be hard to exaggerate either the quality or the quantity of work that has been done. People seem to think we have vast numbers of staff who fly around in helicopters! Oxfam has penetrated communities in the Eastern Province far more deeply than ever before. For Pushpanath, the Regional Representative, this has been one of the miracles of his career. The Lusaka staff from the very start has been determined to integrate relief work with recovery work. They hope that the inroads they have made will serve Oxfam well in the years ahead.'

[6] K. Pushpanath, 'Disaster without Memory: Oxfam's drought programme in Zambia 1992-3', *Development in Practice*, 4, 2, 1994, 81-91.
http://www.developmentinpractice.org/readers/Advocacy/Advocacy%20Pushpanath.pdf

A House in Zambia

telecommunications networks were not sufficiently developed. This was unfortunate, for in other ways 250 Zambezi Road might have proved an ideal regional centre, reflecting its earlier links with the ANC and the Simons.

Although during the second half of my career with Oxfam, as a land rights adviser, I had a number of extremely interesting engagements with the Zambia office, especially on the Copperbelt where Anne Mumbi did some really outstanding work[7], for me it never had quite the same magic as during those eight years when I had the great privilege of working with some of the people who are telling their stories in this collection, dedicated with much love and affection to the memories of Susie Smith and of Jack and Ray Simons.

Robin Palmer, 2006

---

7   I was fortunate to be a member of the 1998 team, together with Michelo Hansungule and Patricia Feeney, which wrote a *Report on Land Tenure Insecurity on the Zambian Copperbelt* http://www.oxfam.org.uk/resources/learning/landrights/downloads/full1998_landtenureinsecurityreport.pdf
    I was equally fortunate to be present at the launch, in March 2004, of the Copperbelt Land Rights Centre in Kitwe.

12. BUYING 250 ZAMBEZI ROAD FOR OXFAM, 1990-92

Robin Palmer

My 'Report on visit to Zambia to buy a property for Oxfam in May 1990' began 'A Desk Officer's life is endlessly varied...' Indeed, it was.

First option to buy

On 20 February 1990, I got a phone call from a friend in Lusaka, Hugh Macmillan, a former history colleague at the University of Zambia, and a long-standing friend of the Simons – and a contributor to this collection (chapter 2). Hugh told me that the Simons were about to sell their property in Lusaka and return home to Cape Town in the light of rapid political changes in South Africa.[1] They were shortly leaving for Cape Town, would return to Lusaka in May to complete exit formalities and then, after decades in exile, finally hope to return home in June. They asked whether Oxfam would be interested in purchasing the whole 250 Zambezi Road compound. According to Dorothy Chikula, Oxfam's Administrator, who was also a friend of the Simons, 'they wanted to give Oxfam something akin to a first option.'

It happened that Susie Smith came in just as I had finished talking to Hugh. She and I both felt very strongly that Oxfam should certainly jump at the chance of buying the whole compound for c.£140,000, given the escalating office and housing rents in Lusaka. I talked to David Bryer, then Overseas (International) Director, who thought we should go for it in principle as we were likely to be committed in Zambia over a long future time span.

---

[1] Jack Simons later recalled: 'When de Klerk made his announcement on February the second, Ray and I on the same day went to the ANC and said, we want to go back home. It took us some time to persuade the African National Congress to give us permission; because we are members, we didn't want to act anarchistically. We wanted to go back with the permission of the ANC and they gave it to us. From the outset, our ambition has been to come back here and take part in what is going on - in the fulfillment of our aims.' Interview with Ray Alexander and Jack Simons, *http://www.sacp.org.za/main.php?include=docs/biography/2006/rjsimon.html*
But in chapter 2, Hugh Macmillan reveals a somewhat more dramatic version of events.

But could Oxfam buy a house? Lightning research by Izzy Birch, the Zambia Desk Administrator, indicated that the precedents for Oxfam owning property were in Addis Ababa and Nairobi (where we bought and sold in the 1970s, and now regretted having sold). So I went to Hugh Belshaw, the Finance Director, to ask for his reaction. I expected a long battle and, in all likelihood, a refusal. But after about fifteen minutes of banding around a few figures of rental costs in Lusaka, Hugh said, 'yes, fine, go ahead.'

Oxfam's staff in Lusaka shared our strong enthusiasm that this was a one-off situation to which we should certainly respond positively and quickly; they had been a little anxious about the reaction in Oxford.

Dorothy Chikula wrote to me a week later, saying that Ray Simons had been unaware that it would be necessary for Oxfam to get state consents etc. 'She thought one could buy property like one buys a car.' Dorothy stressed that:

> *we have to do things properly otherwise Oxfam would end up losing everything back to the state. Oxfam's interests have to be carefully considered and protected. After speaking to the lawyer, it was clear to me that there are no short-cuts in property purchasing especially by an organisation such as ours with integrity to uphold.*

A little later, reflecting on how pompous and condescending officials in high places could be, she urged me to 'bring a suit for such negotiations; they won't take you seriously otherwise.' So I did as I was told.

To Lusaka with Power of Attorney, May 1990

I went out to Zambia from 1-19 May, armed with a Power of Attorney, to try to seal the deal. The timing was conditioned by the Simons' movements, but was extremely unfortunate. On 25 April 'the Charity Commissioners dropped a bombshell on Oxfam', in Maggie Black's words,[2] when they announced their enquiry into Oxfam's campaigning activities - specifically its call for sanctions against apartheid South Africa. This was on the eve of Oxfam's Frontline Africa campaign.

Today such a house sale in Lusaka can be conducted relatively swiftly and with a minimum of foreign exchange complications. But in 1990 things were very different; there were rigid foreign exchange rules in place. The

---

2   Maggie Black, *A Cause for our Times: Oxfam: the first 50 years* (Oxford, Oxfam 1992), 278.

basic dilemma was how to ensure that the Simons could receive money from the sale in hard currency[3] (rather than have it locked up in the notoriously long Bank of Zambia 'pipeline') so that they could buy a flat in Cape Town, whilst at the same time obeying the very stringent Zambian exchange control regulations, so that there would be no possibility of any subsequent legal problems for Oxfam.

There were basically two possible ways of proceeding. The Simons' bank was urging the illegal approach, viz. to declare an 'official' sale price of £60,000 to the Zambian authorities and for Oxfam to make an undeclared payment of £80,000 to the Simons. The alternative, urged by John Jearey (a lawyer recommended to me both by friends in the business world and some of the Simons' friends as a 'painstaking stickler'), was to declare the full price and make a direct appeal to the Zambian authorities for the money to be remitted outside in view of the Simons' age, their contribution to Zambia and the liberation of South Africa, and of Oxfam's good track record in Zambia and our long-term commitment to the country. There were obvious advantages, and obvious drawbacks, with both options.

The problem was compounded by the fact that a new Governor of the Bank of Zambia, Jacques Bussières, had recently and humiliatingly been imposed on Zambia by the IMF as a 'Mr Clean' in an attempt to sweep away corruption.

John Jearey persuaded the Simons to adopt the second option, saying that he couldn't put his signature to documents which he knew contained false figures, and 'you taught me too well, Professor Simons' – he had been his student in Cape Town. So we lobbied a variety of people in the banks, in the political arena and in State House. Both the Simons and I wrote to Jacques Bussières and to President Kaunda. The advice from our mole in State House was to come back to KK only if we received an unfavourable response from the Governor. It was better for the Governor to decide alone; we should deploy the President – who was certain to be sympathetic, we were assured – only as a court of final appeal. This seemed good advice.

---

3 Jack and Ray wrote to me on 1 March 1990, saying 'we wish to make it clear that we are definitely looking for the purchase price in hard currency.'

A House in Zambia

Meeting the Bank Governor

With some trepidation, I went with the Simons to see Governor Bussières on 17 May. I made a brief, well rehearsed, presentation of our case, stressing the Simons' track record and how much Oxfam brought into Zambia each year in foreign exchange (c.£500,000), and appealed for him to adopt a long term view, to use his powers of discretion, and to show a spirit of generosity.

He was very friendly and relaxed and our prior lobbying had obviously had some effect. He said that the Simons would have to bring the whole £140,000 into Zambia for conversion into Kwacha, but that they should write to him documenting their immediate financial requirements for resettling in South Africa (this they did; it came to c.£80,000) and he would allow that amount to be taken out of Zambia promptly. He would ensure that the balance was remitted over a period of months, rather than years. They would not suffer, he said. He couldn't agree to the whole amount going out at once, but was looking for a defensible middle ground. He would treat them as a unique case. I think that he saw the justice of the Simons' case and would probably have conceded everything but for fear of setting a precedent; he said that he didn't want there to be any rumours about the Simons.

Following that meeting, we were able to go back to John Jearey on 18 May to sign a contract by which the Simons agreed to sell to Oxfam for £140,000. The completion date was fixed 'on or before twenty one (21) days from receipt of the State's Consent to Assign', i.e. after the completion of all the legal requirements, searches etc. Jearey said that 'with a fair wind' this might take up to six months.

Oxfam was to continue as tenant of one house until completion; vacant possession of the remainder would be given to Oxfam on 1 July until completion in return for a monthly rent of £622 (8% of two-thirds of the purchase price). Critically, 'the purchase price will be paid in Zambian currency at the market window rate ruling at completion.' A transfer tax of 5% of the full value would have to be paid to the Lands Department by the Simons for consent to the transfer and certificate of title. On 4 June Oxfam was registered as a foreign company in Zambia so that it was legally able to own property. Oxfam would need to get permission from the District Governor to be allowed to use a house in a residential area, Roma, as an office. Jearey pointed out, correctly, that this should prove a formality as the flight of offices out of the city centre was already well underway. In May 1991 Oxfam formally moved its office to 250 Zambezi Road.

Complications

What happened over the next two years was deeply unfortunate and the source of a good deal of understandable angst on the part of the Simons, despite the hard work of people like Hugh Macmillan and Joel Joffe (an Oxfam Trustee with strong ANC links) who sought valiantly to act as intermediaries and honest brokers between the Simons and Oxfam.

So the money had to be sent from a British bank, deposited in a Zambian bank, be converted into Kwacha at the current exchange rate, then make its slow progress through the exchange control pipeline, before coming out the other end, much devalued, before it could be converted back into forex and remitted to Jack and Ray's external bank account. There were bureaucratic complications and some faulty figures from the Lands Department, and the Simons arguably chose the wrong option in contesting these. So it dragged on and when the money was finally released in October, devalued by a significant amount, the Simons, not unnaturally, were furious.

At one time I found myself confronted by one of the most formidable trade union leaders anywhere (Ray) seemingly holding me personally responsible for what had happened; at another they threatened to sue Oxfam. The question was, could Oxfam make up the difference? I felt very strongly that we had a moral obligation to do so,[4] as did Hugh Belshaw. But Frank Judd, Oxfam's Director, was understandably nervous with the Charity Commissioners breathing down his neck. He asked for a legal opinion. We got a distinctly unhelpful one, saying that the agreed figure of £140,000 had no legal validity. As I wrote to Ray on 2 October 1990:

> *K8.4m is the maximum price which Oxfam can now legally pay you. Ever since then [August], we have been trying to find legal ways of paying the difference. We have received firm legal advice saying it is*

---

4 I wrote to Hugh Belshaw on 10 September 1990: 'I do not believe that we should exploit bureaucratic bungling in the Zambian Lands Department and an ill-advised choice by the Simons to now simply sign the assignment for K8.4m and subsequently deprive the Simons of that part of an agreed sterling figure which they would thereby lose. To me that would be morally reprehensible.'

not legal for Oxfam to pay you this difference. I and others have been endeavouring to contest this legal view and to stress the primacy of other factors. But, with the Charity Commissioners currently holding an enquiry into Oxfam, it is obvious that our financial and legal advisers will not look kindly on the type of 'quick and easy' solution which might be available to organizations with less scruples than ours. Thus, threats of legal action and high profile public lobbying against Oxfam only reinforce the caution of our advisers who are insisting that we cannot agree to any 'deal' which carries the slightest taint of illegality.

The assignment, at K8.4m, was signed on 8 October 1990. By March the following year I was able to tell Ray that Frank Judd had insisted that 'whatever we do must be absolutely legal under Zambian law' and that Hugh Belshaw had gone back to the Zambian authorities to ask for special dispensation. It took until November 1991 to get a response from the Bank Governor Bussières to the effect that since neither Oxfam nor the Simons were resident in Zambia, neither were subject to exchange control regulations, and therefore the Bank had nothing against Oxfam paying the Simons compensation for losses incurred in the transaction. But there followed months of negotiations over the correct figure of this compensation. Finally, Hugh Belshaw wrote to me on 28 October 1992 saying that the matter was now closed and that the purchase of 250 Zambezi Road had cost Oxfam £140,000.

All these years later, I'd like to offer huge thanks to Hugh Macmillan and to Joel Joffe for their peacemaking roles. Hugh recently noted during the process of writing this book, 'in the end the Simons were reconciled to the fact that Oxfam had acted in good faith but at the time they were understandably very worried about their financial future and that of their family in South Africa.'

The essential point is that Oxfam Zambia acquired *A House in Zambia* with a very particular and very proud history in the liberation struggle for Southern Africa. As many have reflected in this book, the legacy of Jack and Ray Simons had a powerful impact on many of the Oxfam staff who lived and worked in 250 Zambezi Road.

Buying 250 Zambezi Road for Oxfam

Robin Palmer, 1987

PART FOUR:

THE INCREDIBLE OXFAM SUPPORT STAFF

13. DOROTHY CHIKULA (1980-93)

Joining Oxfam in 1980

It is difficult to compress into a few words the experiences of my association of almost fourteen years with Oxfam in general and with 250 Zambezi Road in particular. I joined Oxfam from the parastatal world in May 1980. I was relieved at last to run away from the commercial world where one worked for and with bosses and all that entailed! I was recruited to take over from an English secretary, Frances Young, the wife of the first Oxfam Field Director in Zambia, Martyn Young. Malitino Daka, a Malawian brought up in Zambia, had just completed his probationary period when I joined.

At first, I missed my beautiful office on the tenth Floor of Findeco House (Lusaka's then tallest building; I suspect it still is), with its luxurious carpeting and fancy furniture, which had been replaced by Oxfam's scruffy large room, subsequently demarcated into three – a larger space for Daka and me to share a corner each, the Field Director's office, and a tiny unisex toilet.

I was just settling down when it was time for Martyn to return home because his contract could no longer be extended. It was a very sad day when he left; he had come to love Zambia or was it Africa, because he had just been less than a year in Zambia, after moving the office from Malawi. He broke down and wept and told Daka and me that he did not want to go at all. He could not even allow us to escort him to the airport. We took care of the office until his replacement arrived in the person of Susanna (Susie) Smith.

After working happily with Martyn, who was a gentleman and a good friend to us both, I was sick with anxiety. 'What kind of person was going to replace Martyn, would I be looking for another job soon?' as most men then were in the habit of acquiring lovers from their work places! Martyn came back a couple of months later with Susie and we were all delighted and reassured! Soon we grew a little in number as Wilson Kaonza joined us.

Susie's arrival

When Susie came, we started being introduced to a lot of Oxfam people who became our friends too. We had a lot of happy moments together. Sometimes our families celebrated with us (a lot of juices and jellies) when it was party time to meet visiting Oxfam leaders.

We also experienced hilarious but annoying moments of cultural or language difficulty. One instance comes to mind when Wilson, who was over a year older than Susie and me, and who was also Susie's favourite of the two men, started calling Susie *amai* the same way he addressed me. Susie discovered that amai meant mother. She was not amused. She went to great pains to explain to Wilson that she was not his mother, neither did she like being addressed as mother in the office, or anywhere else. It took me a long time to convince Wilson for him to change his address to Daka's 'Miss Smith' and later to 'Susanna'!

Susie and Dorothy as friends and workmates

Susie was Oxfam's representative and I was her personal assistant, but she was never my boss nor anybody else's boss. She was our team leader. We always went to her with a lot of confidence and hope no matter the problem, work or personal, even wrongdoing. Her kindly disposition allayed any trepidation.

Susie and I came from diverse backgrounds, racial, cultural and even in terms of beliefs, but we still became very great friends. How was this possible? It was possible because Susie was a very real, warm person, who embraced everyone from all walks of life. She welcomed as friends people from the upper class of society, heads of missions and government (including Prime Ministers and Permanent Secretaries), NGOs and others in that upper class. She also sat at table to laugh and enjoy a meal with the lowly of the Zambian working class, like guards, drivers, office messengers and their families. She was happy and at home in a friend's home in Roma, as much as being with another friend in a shanty compound home in the outskirts of Lusaka or in a remote village in Kashinakaji in North-Western Province. When we visited people in the shanty compounds or villages, Susie would dress in appropriate, modest clothes, wrap herself in a *chitenge* wrapper and a headscarf just like those around us. She would eat *nshima* cooked in not so attractive surroundings and drink the locally brewed sweet beer served in traditional cups without making faces. We have lost a great model.

We shared some light moments

Susie and I were born the same year (1951) May and October respectively and so we sometimes enjoyed doing girlish things together. As Oxfam representative, she was on the Prime Minister's list and was often invited to the Prime Minister's office for this or that. I remember when Oxfam was involved in a famine relief programme in Western Province in 1981/2, we would have just arrived at the office and a call from the PS or PM's Office would come for immediate attendance at that office. After struggling with being professional and attending those important meetings and the problems of fending off lusty advances from some men she met there, she decided that she would always take me with her. So we kept a few smart clothes and shoes at the office which we jokingly termed 'the Prime Minister's outfits'! One of those men, who was a notoriously shameless womanizer, tried to persuade us to send either of us per visit, we politely 'convinced' him that we needed two people from Oxfam for the sake of continuity!

The Mbathas and the Simons

Besides the Oxfam friends of Susie, we were privileged to be introduced to Alexander and Khosi Mbatha, South Africans who had been rescued by Oxfam campaigning from South African prisons during the struggle. They became friends of Oxfam and its staff in Zambia too. At the same time, we were introduced to Jack and Ray Simons. I think I became their special friend from the Oxfam office because of my vegetarian diet. Ray would always call me to pass by and get some special dish. She would describe how she had made it and encourage me to try it in my home. She even taught me how to make marmalade from the grapefruit that grew in their yard. Just before they left Zambia and Oxfam acquired their home in 1990, I visited them to discuss bills arising from the properties in the yard, where we rented a house for the Oxfam representative, and which sometimes got mixed up. Ray was having a bath and I found Jack alone. By then his sight was not very good, because after I greeted him and explained why I had come, he looked at me at said, 'you are from the Oxfam office, good, good; you must not forget to convey my special greetings to a very dear friend of ours, who has been with Oxfam for a long time. You work with Dorothy, don't you? She is a very nice person, our legacy, together with Bobby, from our dear friend Susanna. How do you feel about her, is she as nice to you as she is to us?' It was a very difficult conversation. Not wanting to offend Jack, I had to be very careful in my selection of words. When I rose to leave, he stood up and went to call out to Ray, 'Ray, a young woman has been visiting us from the Oxfam office, don't you want to come out and send Dorothy some fruit or something?' When Ray came out, we both pretended that Dorothy was at the office!

Like everybody who worked for Oxfam at the time, we all met the Doctors, Nurses etc at 250 Zambezi, but apart from Alex and Khosi, whom I later visited in their home in Ammersfoot, Holland, back in 1988, I didn't get close to the others.

Dr Edwards

Mike Edwards came to replace Susie in 1984. The men (Daka and Wilson) liked to refer to him as Dr Edwards when he wasn't listening (he preferred to be called simply Mike by everybody), because it made them feel important to be daily associating with someone with such a title. Before he left, Mike also extended our office family, with the recruitment of Lucy Muyoyeta, Christine Chinzewe, Felix Chiputa and later on Francis Banda. We were now a big family with attendant challenges of growth. Mike will remember Dux Halubobya, the CUSA Chief Executive and landlord of CUSA building, where we rented offices. He is now both a businessman and commercial farmer in Lusaka. One thing Dux detested about Mike was his simple snack for his daily lunch, which he bought a few metres from the office, came back and ate in the office. Dux appreciated directors who went out to some 'respectable' place to have their meal; we were next to Big 5 travel agents and several FAO offices upstairs. As a result of this resentment, he never really took the trouble to learn Mike's name. He would refer to him as Dr Lloyd-Williams (mixing him up with Anne who had stood in for a couple of months, after Susie left and before Mike came), or Dr Edward Smith-William, or simply the young doctor! He also frequently asked me to do something about my boss's lunch arrangements. We said nothing to Mike; this was a secret among the staff!

Push and Uma

After Mike, came Push with his lovely family in 1988. Push stood out as the most generous Rep we ever had. We used to look forward to his home leave or out of country visits, because he would always bring lots of presents indiscriminately (regardless of the level of friendship) for each one of us; clothes, makeup, chocolates and other goodies. Remember, this was still during

Zambia's long phase of shortages of essential and even non-essential commodities. One had to have forex to taste an apple or such categorized luxuries! I must admit, though, that I instantly became more of Uma's friend than Push's. I often took my little daughter, who was the same age as their youngest son, to play with their boys at 250 Zambezi and even when they moved to Kabulonga. While the kids amused themselves, Uma taught me how to prepare different types of vegetarian dishes and gave me several recipes too. Up to now people say I am a very good cook! She also introduced me to different types of herbs and how to use them effectively in cooking. I was very sad to see her leave together with the children, but thank God that I had had the privilege to meet such a truly lovely, warm and friendly person.

Susie, her friends, pregnancy and sterilization

Susie had a wide circle of friends and she endeavoured to introduce all to us, her office family. I will just pick a few of those who made lasting impressions on my life. Gabriel Banda is still a friend of the family; he has always endeavoured to keep me abreast with the happenings around Oxfam circles, happy moments and even sad ones. Then there were Dr Tony Klouda, Peter Wiles and Peter Lee. I had been struggling with birth control methods due to my endless allergies, but I could not find any really suitable pills etc. So I said to Frank, my husband, that I had done more than my quota of birth control, it was high time he came in and did his part. Susie said 'tell Tony (Klouda) about it' and I wrote to him. Tony gave a detailed contribution from a medical viewpoint, giving various options and advice. Convincing Frank took too long and I got pregnant again for the second time, while faithfully swallowing the pills and a copper loop inserted!

The doctors had done all in their power to prevent pregnancy, so the pregnancy test was not even at the bottom of their list. The clinic called me to receive their latest results. Frank was out of town. Susie offered to accompany me to the clinic and I thanked God that she did, because I discovered that I was pregnant! Susie held me comfortingly and reassuringly encouraged me not to panic. I have never forgotten that experience.

The baby was born prematurely in the seventh month. The two Peters who were in Lusaka actually came home to see the baby. We (but the men really) had a very interesting discussion as the Peters coaxed and encouraged Frank to get sterilized! They seemed to have satisfactorily persuaded him for he promised to do it 'as soon as it could be arranged'. However, his family and friends managed to change his mind for him, I could not take any more chances and so, when the baby was three months, I ended up being the one that got painfully sterilized!

Buying the property from the Simons
During the protracted purchase of the property from the Simons (1990-92), Push delegated me to act as link messenger between the Oxfam office and the lawyers, a Mr John Jearey. On first contact with his office, intimidating-type secretary and all, I was secretly happy to note I was not seeking services for either my prosecution or defence! As the interaction continued I became more comfortable and was able to exchange messages easily. When the purchase was finalised, I also felt a high sense of achievement, though of course the visible glory rightly went to Push, as Oxfam's Rep.

Nawina
As we settled in nicely as owners of 250 Zambezi Road, a very bubbly young woman joined Oxfam, Nawina Hamaundu. A very lovely, vibrant individual, she exuded joy and happiness all around, inspired love from all types of people, not only from her husband and children. She enjoyed life to the best of her ability and had no apologies to make, not even in her sometimes unconventional and flamboyant dressing, even when she visited the field. I was truly sorry to learn of the abrupt end of her young life.

Leaving Oxfam
250 Zambezi was not some saintly paradise, so some of the good and bad that could possibly happen in a setting of more than one person happened. The experience that I perceived to be the worst was my exit. Though my association with 250 Zambezi was largely a very happily memorable experience, my exit was not.

Friday 18 October 1993 started as a normal day. There was a lot of excitement in the office with people coming and going. But at 16.15 I was invited to a meeting. By 16.30 my job was gone. I had been sacked and told to clear my desk, pack and leave. I had anticipated that I would be retired the following January and given proper written notice of three months. So this was deeply shocking.

It took the Church, family and friends four months to rebuild my self-worth and enough confidence to apply for another job. But this turned out to be a blessing in disguise, as these past thirteen years which the human mind told me were going to be lean years, turned out to be years of plenty, with much reflection for me. I have come to realise that no one did wrong or was better than others, we all, consciously or unconsciously, simply contributed to a situation which went haywire. For me, the experiences (good and bad) and exposure have worked together to produce a wiser Dorothy and I thank everyone who touched my life, in whatever way, all those years ago.

The Christian Bible in Romans 8.28 counsels thus: 'And we know that all things work together for good to them that love God.' As we all reminisce on the old times we shared with all our friends, living and departed, let's thank God (or whatever we believe in) that we are still alive and healthy to share that part of our lives with others. May I share a little song, that I have found very encouraging over the years:

'Though the road is often rough and stony,
Though the hills are often steep and wide,
You can wear a smile and keep on singing,
Never let your courage die!'
Chorus
'Oh don't let the song go out of your heart,
No matter, how dark the day ...eh..eh..eh!
Oh don't let the song go out of your heart,
Your troubles will soon, pass away...'

Susie's death – and some memories

Susie's death came in June 2006 as a great shock to me, to my family and our mutual larger family of friends and relatives. We had all known her as a very warm, friendly, polite person. I am very sorry for myself that I did not get a chance to pay my last respects to a very dear friend. But she has left us so many very good memories. For example, when I arrived at the Oxford train station in November 1999 looking for a blond Susie with shoulder length hair, I missed her because she was wearing a dark grey short (afro-like) wig! I don't know what she was looking for, but she also missed me because I had a black weave and did not look 48! We had such a long

A House in Zambia

laugh later and I think Sarah, her daughter, listening to us thought we were a bunch of idiotic mothers!

Susie and I always discussed issues related to my Christian beliefs. She refused to be converted. She would lift up her hands in protest, 'please Dorothy, do not try to convert me!' But she would still sit and listen to me talk about the things I had done in my life and that of my family. I remember the time when her mother Prudence had been very sick back in 1988, she did not object when I offered to pray for Prue for the two weeks I spent in her home. Knowing how I felt about Prue's illness I was pleasantly surprised when Susie called me and informed me later that Prue had been healed, believing that 'Dorothy's God had answered our prayers.' She informed me that Prue had consequently embraced and converted to the Christian faith as a Quaker, 'which is easier than being an Adventist' and had even changed her Will to embrace the Christian burial when her time came.

Dorothy Chikula, 2008

Dorothy Chikula

Oxfam Zambia team, 1987. The team that Susie and Mike built:
Back: Dorothy Chikula, Felix Chiputa, Caroline Allison (regional), Francis Banda, Christine Chinzewe.
Front: Wilson Kaonza, Lucy Muyoyeta, Sara Makrani (regional), Malitino Daka

A House in Zambia

Dorothy Chikula in Oxfam House, 1988

14. MALITINO DAKA (1980-98)

Joining Oxfam
I joined Oxfam on 17 March 1980 as Clerk/Messenger. I had come across the advert in the papers, applied for the job and was called for an interview, which proved successful. I was the first local person to be employed by the late Martyn Young, Director of the Lusaka office.

I have seen Oxfam grow. When I joined Oxfam in Lusaka, it was only a one roomed office at Pioneer House, owned by Credit Union and Savings Association of Zambia, CUSA. Pioneer House was along Cairo Road. In that one roomed office there was a partition between where the Director was occupying and the other space, the front part, which we shared with the secretary, who was also the wife of Martyn Young. Mrs Dorothy Chikula later joined us to become the secretary, taking over from Frances Young.

Susanna Smith
I worked under the management of the late Martyn Young. Thereafter came the tall late Susanna Smith, may her soul rest in eternal peace, whom I worked and associated with extremely well, under minimum supervision.

In terms of projects or programmes we supported, they were the best that Oxfam funded in Zambia during my working with Oxfam. Susanna is the one who initiated support and funding of projects in far flung places in remotest rural Zambia, where poverty levels are always extremely high. This is the greatest achievement and legacy that Susanna Smith left behind after leaving Zambia in 1984.

Later on came the energetic Michael Edwards, followed by Puspanath and Lucy Muyoyeta.

Moving to 250 Zambezi Road
In those days, Oxfam was not allowed to own property in Zambia. I played a role when arrangements were being made in 1990 to buy the property at 250 Zambezi Road, Roma Township. I was often at the National Commission for Development Planning (NCDP), delivering correspondence between the government and Oxfam. Robin Palmer was crucial. He was the main person who brokered the agreement with NCDP. Robin came over to Lusaka to sign the agreement (see chapter 12).

A House in Zambia

The Resource Centre

At 250 Zambezi Road, I was made in charge of and created the Resource Centre. The Resource Centre idea was brought up by the project implementers themselves in order to be empowered with knowledge and experiences in other developed or developing countries that have made successes in projects they run. The Book Token Scheme was the tool which helped so much to source books from Oxfam free of charge. Oxfam Lusaka office, Oxfam partners and researchers benefited so much, as Gabriel Banda has shown in chapter 18. Susanna Smith, then working in Oxford, deeply supported this initiative of having a Resource Centre and, as Robin Palmer has noted in chapter 11, 'Oxfam sent people from other parts of Southern Africa to Lusaka to look at the model Daka had established.' It made me very sad to learn, after I left employment in May 1998, that the Centre became no more, a sad development indeed.

In May 1998 I was made redundant. It is now exactly ten years out of formal employment and I have fended for myself and family by being self-employed as a small trader and have sustained myself up to today. I run the 'Fairer World' shop at Lusaka's Mtendere Market.

I would like to thank the Almighty God for keeping me alive and wisdom to look after myself and the large family in my custody. Despite some setbacks, I still wish Oxfam well for future activities and programmes both in Zambia and in the UK.

Malitino Daka, 1987

15. WILSON KAONZA (1981-96)

Joining Oxfam in 1981

I started work with Oxfam on 4 April 1981. At that time, the Field Director of Oxfam in Zambia and Malawi was Susanna Smith. I was the first person to be employed as a driver in the Oxfam office. At the time of Susanna, at the office we were three workers, Mrs Dorothy Chikula, Malitino Daka, and I. Susanna, from Oxford in the UK, was the fourth.

Susanna's work in Zambia

Susanna and I travelled all over Zambia. Our first trip was to Livingstone, with Susanna's mother, Prudence Smith. We were going to a project in Sesheke. On this journey, when Susanna met people in the villages, in all meetings she told people that we had come to the area so that we could all learn from one another about the problems and challenges being faced in the villages. She said we had not come with a lot of money but we needed to teach one another about removing problems in our villages.

Here, I saw that Susanna wanted first to learn together with people in finding ways of dealing with the problems people were facing in their villages and communities. She also wanted to work together with the community and not have the community members consider every visitor as coming with money. And because of someone in a project in Kanyama, Lusaka, who, after getting some money, disappeared and was not seen again, Susanna became very careful in her work.

There was one trip when we went to Mongu. When we reached Lyambai Hotel, Susanna told me to get my bag and find accommodation. I refused to go by foot and leave the motor vehicle at Lyambai. I said I could not go on foot to Namushakende or Limulunga, which was a distance of some six kilometres. When Susanna heard my words, she said she would drive me to the rest house and collect me in the morning. I thought Susanna was understanding of others' difficulties. She used to do many things to help others. This did not happen to me only, but to anyone in difficulties.

Then there was another trip to Chipata. Zithandizeni Nutrition Group was being led by Mrs Margaret Lungu and the Danish Volunteer Service, DVS. When we reached Katete, Susanna was feeling very sick. We went to St. Francis Hospital. Susanna was in the hospital for one day. When she was discharged, I said that we should go back to Lusaka. But Susanna said she was fit to go and visit the project and that people there were waiting for her.

After we finished the visit to Zithandizeni, Susanna started off for Mfuwe (with the Danish volunteers) in the Luangwa Game Park. I remained in Chipata. But before they reached Mfuwe, they had a road accident. They came out unhurt. We went and towed the vehicle and brought it to Chipata garage.

We made many tours with Susanna and travelled to many parts of Zambia and Malawi. Susanna would eat anything offered in the villages and communities. But if there was one thing Susanna refused to take, it was kapenta (dried fish). She used to say that, in the plate, kapenta's two eyes would look at you. So she used to decline eating kapenta but would eat everything else. And Susanna used to like to sleep in the villages. She had great love for people.

Robin Palmer

After some time, another senior person Robin Palmer, a professor, visited the Zambia office. He and I travelled around Zambia and Malawi. He was observing how projects were going in Zambia and Malawi. He also had love for all of us.

Mike Edwards' time

Mike Edwards was a person I travelled with around Zambia and Malawi. Mike helped change the way projects by the Catholics were running, and saw that people in communities did development activities by themselves. It happened in Chipata, in other areas in Zambia, and in Malawi, with projects dealing with farming as a way of removing hunger.

Pushpanath's time

With Push, I moved around Zambia and Malawi a lot. Push was a person who did not like to find one person marginalising others in projects or politics. His behaviour was different from that of many of Asian origin found in Zambia. He did not have Indian friends in Zambia.

Push used to work together with persons in projects where Oxfam was. He used to drink alcohol like a true Zambian! Push was not jealous of people he was with in the Oxfam office. He did not show others that he was the boss. He got on well with everyone at the office.

Lucy Muyoyeta's time

Lucy Muyoyeta was the first Zambian Oxfam Country Representative. We worked very well with Lucy. With her, we also travelled around Zambia, Malawi, and Niassa province in northern Mozambique. She was a lady who liked a lot to meet the women in the communities. She was running Oxfam very well.

Later, she told me Oxfam wanted to retrench some workers in UK and Zambia.[1] I was the first one to be made redundant. I agreed to be retrenched. This was in 1996. But the payments did not go well. We ended up going to courts. But we did not have money to pay lawyers and we failed in our case. Here, Oxfam marginalised us. We should have been helped with the issue of redundancy package in Oxfam.[2]

Rest in peace, Susanna

In October 2004, I heard, on the phone, that Susanna was in Zambia. At that time, I was in the office of Francis Banda, former Oxfam staff.

In 2006, I heard about the death of Susanna. I, Wilson Kaonza, say may Susanna's body rest in peace, in the name of Jesus Christ. These are my ending words.

---

1 There were external pressures on Lucy at this time, from unsympathetic sources in Oxford, to 'downsize' the Lusaka staff. Those responsible had little understanding of the history and extremely high calibre of the staff they were retrenching.
2 Note by Robin Palmer: whilst undoubtedly heartfelt by Wilson, it seems unrealistic to expect Oxfam to pay the legal fees of former staff who were in effect suing them.

A House in Zambia

Wilson Kaonza, 1987

16. LAZAROUS CHEWE (1989-95)

My experience with Oxfam is very interesting.[1] I joined the Oxfam family in 1989 when I was a very, very small kid. I was about twenty years, just from school. There was a vacancy. They wanted somebody to help them with the office work at the time. So I went to Oxfam.

Learning about development

So one of the things I learnt was that Oxfam was basically involved in development. And it was a very interesting experience in the sense that, as a young man, I had an opportunity to learn because philosophically Oxfam tried to help the staff to understand the programmes that they were involved in.

And it is during this time that I started having a lot of interest in the work that Oxfam was doing. I was heavily involved in community projects and I took advantage of the things that I found in Oxfam in the very interesting Resource Centre. So I could see a lot of students coming from the University of Zambia. They would come and get information. So I started getting interested because I had just completed my school. I started reading a lot of materials and really that was the beginning of my realisation. I started really appreciating development.

At one time, Pushpanath, the Regional Representative, decided to leave the house he was living in at 250 Zambezi Road. So the owners of that place (Jack and Ray Simons) decided that I remain at the place to look after it. So I continued working but Oxfam was paying me because the house in which Push had been living was still being paid for by Oxfam. So I was looking after the house and doing all the works that Oxfam was doing.

Looking after 250 Zambezi Road

I remember vividly Jack Simons, who was a professor, and his wife was Ray. They wanted me to help them with the maintenance of the place and assigned general duties to me.

At that place there was a policy that nobody was allowed to cut grass. So it was quite bushy. So people were wondering whether there were people living

---

1 Lazarous Chewe told his story to Gabriel C Banda in September 2007. He asked Gabriel to do some minor editing and re-sequencing. It has been further edited by Robin Palmer.

there because it is quite a big place and nobody was allowed to cut any grass. You couldn't cut any tree. So the Simons were very environmentally conscious.

Now, one day, I made a mistake. I was walking around the yard and then I spotted a snake. It was a very big snake. It was brown. So you know I got scared. What comes into my mind? I decided to confront that snake. I killed that snake. To me, I felt what I had done was good because the snake was dangerous. So I took that snake to Professor Jack Simons. I said, 'Jack, I've killed a snake!' But he got annoyed with me and said, 'suppose I took off your head, how you would feel?'

So he explained to me that you don't kill these things, it was a harmless snake. Then I felt bad. I felt bad to myself because at that time I didn't realise the importance of these creatures because God has created these things and they have the right to live. So, from that experience, it has always been in my mind. It lingers in my mind every time I remember that incident.

Then I remember that during 1990 Oxfam started negotiating to purchase that place. And because every time Pushpanath, our Regional Representative, talked about it in the meetings we used to have, I, as small as I am, concurred with him, that we needed to buy it.

One thing I remember is that we had a meeting. You know Oxfam worked with community groups, so I remember we had a meeting of partners. It used to be called the Advisory Group. It was a meeting comprising community representatives where Oxfam was running programmes. At my age I was given the responsibility to organise the people and the participants. So I remember I organised them, I brought them, and I was the one who was involved in the buying of the mattresses, and the food that they were going to eat. I also participated in the cooking of the food for the delegates.

So it is from that background that the interest to have that place as our own developed because we had developed that relationship with the Simons who were living there. And I think from that time, a lot of people now came in. Robin Palmer, I remember him coming. He also expressed interest and generally the people at the office also wanted 250 Zambezi Road to be theirs. So in 1990 Oxfam bought that property and moved its office there in May 1991.

Now, before the Simons left that place, I think a lot of people did not understand some things. You know that it was an ANC base. I was privileged to that information because I stayed there. So I had a lot of interaction with people from South Africa. Some of them were guerrillas. Some carried guns but they were very peaceful people and they were revolutionary. They were involved in the freedom struggle. So I managed with a lot of different people.

A remarkable visitor

One day, in February 1990, Professor Simons approached me and said, 'Lazarus this evening I want you to be closer to the gate. We are expecting some people so ensure that when they come you allow them to come in.' So I said, 'okay'. And around 18:00 hours, I heard a horn at the gate. So I went to see who was at the gate. I saw two vehicles, one was a Peugeot 504. You remember that at that time a Peugeot was a car of the moment.

I saw that there was a Peugeot and a Fiat. Now the Fiat was bearing a GRZ (government) number plate. So I opened the gate. Then people came in with the cars. I closed that gate. Then I saw six people come out of the vehicle. There was this one, an African who was light, an old man. I decided to just walk around. I saw the Professor coming from the house. He shouted 'Nelson!'. Then I wondered, 'why is he shouting?' Then these two old people, Jack Simons and the tall African man, hugged each other. They were near the elephant sculpture on the verandah. And I could see that the old tall man was crying.

Now I got inquisitive. I wanted to know why he was crying. So I stood at the distance, watching. I saw those people crying for about three good minutes. Then they went into the house. And I went to the driver of the vehicle. I asked him, 'why is the old man crying?' He said, 'no that was Nelson Mandela, he has come to see the Professor.'

They spent about thirty minutes to one hour in the house. Then I saw them come out and I compared to what I saw in the newspaper because I never knew Mandela but from the newspapers that I was reading in the office. Then I said, 'yes, I think that is Nelson Mandela.'

So that is the only contact I remember, that was the closest memory I have of Nelson Mandela and Jack Simons. I think the rest was history. And it is from that background that I was privileged to meet Mandela at the same 250 Zambezi Road at Oxfam. After he was released from prison, the first country he came to was Zambia. From 1990, when Mandela was released from prison, it was a period when the struggle in South Africa really reached a climax.

My exposure to Oxfam

Now another interesting part was when these ANC people repatriated, they gave me a lot of books. There were books on women. There were a lot of books on socialism and just philosophical books. I never bothered to read those books until now (in the 2000s), that is when I use them. Now I understand that, but that time I couldn't relate much to them.

That was over 15 years ago. Now I have experienced, I have increased my levels of education and now as a Rastafarian I read a lot of philosophy. I have really come to realise that actually those people were very serious educators and it is through Oxfam that I got this kind of information and exposure. I think for me it has been a very, very good learning experience. The information that I got from Zambezi Road at Oxfam! I think of all the people that have been there, I don't think there is anybody who has gained more than I have gained from my experience at Oxfam. It is a very huge experience and I use it in my work.

Because I was exposed to development work, it has just married into what I am doing now. I am running programmes that are community based. So I use a lot of information from books that I got from the Simons and from the exposure that I got from Oxfam. And I think that has made me to be a solid individual and, really, although we had our own misunderstandings, I think it's a very interesting experience.

And I hope other people that are working, who even if in terms of position might have small positions, should understand Oxfam philosophically. It is a very good organisation, although some people would come in and start disturbing things. But I think in terms of what it stands for, it is a very, very good organisation to work with. One can learn a lot.

Leaving Oxfam

Well actually it's very interesting because I was retrenched at Oxfam at the age of twenty six. I remember my Regional Representative summoned me into her office. Then I was told that due to the restructuring taking place in Oxfam, my services were no longer required. I remember that even at the age of 26, I had a lot of zeal. They told me they wished there was a way we could do it, but that was the scenario.

But I ended up addressing them, I said, 'No, you see, when you are born, you must realise that one day you will die. So to me, I have been working for Oxfam for the last six years. So it is time for me to move on.' So I thanked them for giving me that opportunity. I was paid my benefits, although there was some grievance on my benefits and perhaps because of maybe just misunderstanding and the way sometimes people approach issues, it wasn't done according to what I expected. But, that aside, I moved ahead.

After Oxfam – working as a taxi driver, paying for my education and a job with Care

From Oxfam I bought a car and I turned it a taxi. So from my experience, because Oxfam had already empowered me, I knew how to drive. I knew I had some money. I paid for my education. I started pursuing a diploma in marketing. So I decided I will go on. I started moving but things couldn't move according to my liking.

What happened was I faced some challenges. Just coming from a formal employment is difficult but I managed. I stayed in that business for about two to three years. Now I was also doing my studies. I decided to apply for jobs. I couldn't get a job so what I did was, somebody told me that there was a job vacancy at Care International. So I asked them what job is there and they said they were looking for a driver.

I asked what programme was there? 'There is a stove project.' So I decided to go to Care International. I applied as a driver but I had a Diploma in Marketing. What I wanted was a job. So I started driving people around but they didn't realise that I had a Diploma in Marketing. Now when I was doing this work at Care, I also made an impact. My knowledge about development was so deep, so the Project Manager started querying because I would advise them on how to approach communities because most of the people who were employed had just come from University. They didn't have skill in teaching methodology, so they had problems. So I could help them so they started wondering how a driver can be so knowledgeable about development. So what happened was the programme was designed to promote improved stoves biomass energy vision stoves in Zambia. Unfortunately, the Care programme couldn't move. They failed to secure money for marketing activities. So that stove project came to an end.

Starting my own enterprise, working on biomass technology, and recording music

Then I also went back onto the street. I couldn't find a job, but this time I looked at the experience that I had gained and my academic skills. Then I decided this time to start my own enterprise. So I registered a company. It was called Dread &Works Enterprises. This is a community project that is basically designed to promote biomass technology.[2]

I have done a lot of research. In Zambia I can boast that I am one of the people that understand energy efficient technology. So what we do is we train communities in how to make energy efficient stoves. I have applied to the National Institute for Scientific Research to give us a working place, where we can take these technologies. Dr Lewanika has given us a go ahead.

In 2005, I also did a programme in China. I went to train at the University of Sichuan, where I came out with a diploma certificate in construction of biomass digesters.

I am also privileged to sit on a SADC board which is a professional board that advises government ministries on rural energy technologies. I am one of the people that have been elected to be part of the steering committee for bio-gas energy promotion in Africa.

One of the things I am going to do next year, God willing, is to start a degree at the Open University on Development Studies.

I have also developed myself. I am a musician. I also play music so I will be performing. We have a reggae concert. So if you hear someone called Holy Man just know that it's me. I have done about three songs and we are still recording. But ideally what I intend to do is to record in Zambia and then go and mix my work in South Africa. So, if I am on course, I will be able to have an album next year.

These are some of the things that I have gone through. But otherwise, to me, Zambezi Road Oxfam is my baby.

---

2 For details of the proposed installation of a demo biogas digester in Lilanda compound see *https://www.biogasafrica.org/News/Pages/DreadWorksEnterpriseinstallsdemo-biogasdigesterinLilanda,Zambia.aspx*

Lazarous Chewe

Lazarous Chewe, 1994

Lazarous Chewe, 2005

17. VICTOR PELEKAMOYO (1992-97)

First impressions of Oxfam

I arrived at 250 Zambezi Road in a taxi for what was supposed to be a job interview for a consultant accountant to work on the drought programme in the Eastern Province of Zambia. Oxfam had just embarked in 1992 on an unprecedented drought response programme during Southern Africa's worst drought in fifty years and they were looking for someone to strengthen the capacity of their partners and communities in reporting, record keeping and accounting for donor and Oxfam funds. I had never done this sort of thing before as most of it was as we later came to coin 'social accounting' – accountable, simple and responsive.

Frankly, I had never heard of Oxfam (UK & Ireland, as it then was) and did not even know of its existence in Zambia until August 1992 when a colleague in Lusaka referred me to the then Regional Representative for Zambia and Malawi, Pushpanath, for a consultancy assignment. I was at this time working for a Lusaka-based quasi non-governmental organisation and would you believe it, one of its donors was actually Oxfam America.

I entered the house through the back to the reception where Jane Mwamba the receptionist/secretary was expecting me. The office was unusually clean, quiet, informal, friendly and most of all modestly furnished. Push came to fetch me from the reception and led me to the Regional Representative's office. It was very small (just enough space for three people) and had old and seemingly cheap furniture - well, for a Regional Representative of an international organisation you expected better. And by the way, typical of accountants and probably most job seekers, I was in my best tie and suit and my host was in jeans, t-shirt and sandals! I felt overdressed for the occasion and I was quite uncomfortable especially when Push made complimentary comments and remarks about it.

On the bus to the Eastern Province

We had an informal chat about the role and my credentials. I was never outrightly offered the assignment but given a challenge to join Push, the late Francis Banda, Wilson Kaonza and two trainee journalists from the UK on a field trip to the Eastern Province. They travelled by car and I had to join them two days later but had to make the journey by public transport -

something I would never have contemplated doing. I was to join them in Katete, which is roughly five hundred kilometres from Lusaka. Armed with a new supply of t-shirts and jeans, I got on the bus at 07:00 am although the bus only started off around 12:00 after all the seats and standing spaces had been occupied. I stood the whole length of the journey and only got to Katete and Mphangwe Motel at 10:00 pm. I was warmly welcomed, showered with food and a lot of Mosi lager.

We spent the following two days in the villages conducting community meetings; we set off in the morning and only got back to the motel late in the afternoon. It was exciting to experience for the very first time the late Francis Size Banda at work, energising the communities and facilitating mass open air meetings and Push, in an attempt not to miss any detail, arguing with the translator to say what the people were saying and not what he thought they were saying. I spent time with the communities and partners talking about records, problems, etc. This was to be my first contact of working hand-in-hand with 'the people' and an out of an office setting.

I had passed the test and was verbally offered the consultancy, although I dreaded the return journey by bus. After a passionate lecture about Oxfam funds and values, Push agreed as a one-off for Oxfam to buy me a return air ticket to Lusaka. I returned to Lusaka on my own in what was only the fourth flight of my life.

This was to mark a start of my long career with Oxfam and a memorable one at that. I was to spend close to four years working at 250 Zambezi Road before moving on to Harare. I maintained very close contact with the office and made regular business and personal visits to the office until 1998, when after a number of unsuccessful recruitments the accountant's role was finally filled. Later most of my colleagues were laid off, retired or moved on.

The transition from Push to Lucy

Lucy Muyoyeta returned to Zambia and her substantive post soon after I had commenced work with Oxfam and she took over as Regional Representative from Push in 1993. The transition was smooth and uneventful – well, apart from Push's farewell party held in the gardens of 250 Zambezi Road. Push subjected us to his version of the Congolese Kwasa Kwasa dance. Anything African, Push's response was Kwasa Kwasa - although to be fair to the dance – he made a mockery of it - he had one monotonous style – continuous wriggle of the waist with a slight lift of the hip.

That said, Push and Lucy provided such remarkable leadership to the Zambia team and helped mould a culture and an identity that is alive in the minds of many today. They reinforced the belief of people-in-people and used resources to better that understanding. One such resource that was easily accessible to people of all backgrounds was 250 Zambezi Road itself. It was so welcoming and simple in character despite its location in an affluent neighbourhood. There are a number of qualities that made 250 Zambezi Road a unique place to work.

An open door policy

During working hours the main gate and front entrance to the office were always left open. In my early days with Oxfam Zambia, I was always amazed by the number and background of visitors that came to 250 Zambezi Road, both announced and unannounced. Both programme and administrative staff were friendly and accommodating to partners and visitors and always found time for them. As an outsider, I wondered why Oxfam laboured so much to make the partners feel that Oxfam existed because of them and not the other way round. I remember arriving at the office early one morning and finding a group of partners camped in the yard after an overnight journey from one of the provincial projects. Although we had been expecting them, we did not expect them to arrive late in the night and come to the office. It was this strong sense of belief, belonging and co-existence between Oxfam and its partners that was undoubtedly the cornerstone of what was to be Oxfam Zambia's reputable relationships. Oxfam Zambia believed in its partners and its partners believed in it. Most importantly, partners felt welcome and wanted whenever they visited 250 Zambezi Road.

Informal meetings

No area of the property was out of bounds. Staff, partners and contacts met on the verandah, under fruit trees, in the Resource Centre - literally anywhere you could feel comfortable to meet. It is this informality that struck a chord with many visitors – imagine a meeting occasionally supplemented with fresh fruit picked from the gardens of 250 Zambezi Road.

Water

Lusaka is a town prone to water supply disruptions and sometimes this could last a long time if not perennial. 250 Zambezi Road was connected to the main council water supply and also had a private borehole in the back so water was not a problem. People as far as Ng'ombe compound came to fetch water and, within reason, they were allowed to fill buckets and plastic containers. We would occasionally have queues of people filling plastic bottles, buckets, etc with water.

I remember being part of the decision to disconnect the council water supply to the property after spiralling water bills and a threat of litigation from the council. A few months later our borehole submersible pump stopped working and we expected severe water supply disruptions to the main office and the two properties in the yard after utilizing all the water stored in the tank. However, water continued flowing long after all our borehole water had been consumed – apparently the property was still connected to the council water supply but we had no clue where the pipe connections were. We continued enjoying 'free water' supplemented by the borehole.

Friday happy hours

Whenever staff were not travelling out of Lusaka, Friday became a day to look forward to. Staff took turns to buy 'drinks' and snacks and after work we all had drinks until late in the night in the peaceful surroundings of 250 Zambezi Road. This was a moment of great fun, much laughter and a time to pour out emotions. It was often at such gatherings that you came to learn one or two things about the property and its famous 'owners', tenants and the history of Oxfam in Zambia. It was the passion and commitment of most long serving staff that was inspiring at such gatherings – you could see it in their eyes as they laboured to explain how they had started off as Oxfam in Zambia, managers under whom they had served and field visits undertaken, etc.

Parties

Parties at 250 Zambezi Road were always memorable – blazing music courtesy of Zambian reggae outfit and Oxfam's partner, Burning Youth, and a lot of wonderful people – staff, partners, etc. I think we always had an excuse for a party every year. My first ever was Lucy's welcome back party – how appropriate.

Victor Pelekamoyo

The people

I have met a lot of people in my life but not all as interesting as the ones I met at 250 Zambezi Road and through its networks. It is the diversity of their backgrounds and experiences that is important to note – bee keepers, farmers, mothers, teachers and lecturers, doctors and nurses, actors and actresses, journalists, researchers, consultants, musicians, civil servants, UN officials, engineers, development workers, church leaders and priests, ordinary men and women, staff and partners. It is not so much the numbers but the frequency of visitors and how the networks grew and concretized into a mass movement of people fighting a common enemy - poverty.

It is no accident nor coincidence, that 250 Zambezi Road is not only iconic but also bears testimony to the magnanimity of what is humanely possible through effort and commitment. It has served men and women of all backgrounds and its legacy is intact although little publicised. It symbolises how collective strength can triumph over adversity.

It is therefore befitting that in the 1980s and 1990s, Oxfam in Zambia continued on the path of extending an open hand to disadvantaged people, groups and organizations and used 250 Zambezi Road as a tool and means to create a level playing field and base for consultations, meetings, fun, much planning and resolute decisions – we hope just as the Simons and the ANC would want to remember the 'place'.

250 Zambezi Road made affluent Roma Township look ordinary.

Victor Pelekamoyo, 2007

PART FIVE:

SOME FRIENDS OF OXFAM

18. 250 ZAMBEZI ROAD - A FRIEND'S VIEW

Gabriel C Banda

As an observer and friend of Oxfam colleagues and their work in Zambia at 250 Zambezi Road, Roma, Lusaka over many years, I can truthfully claim that they helped generate developments in many areas.[1] 250 Zambezi Road was a focal point where people met and the source of some innovative sharing and actions. Oxfam, cooperating and working with others, contributed to developments in Southern Africa and Zambia's NGO and social development environment. Oxfam contributed to values in the development process. From the nourishment of 250 Zambezi Road, our sister Susanna Smith, and those who followed on, contributed to supporting various projects working for the common good.

Just as the 1980s decade started, while doing some theatre for development and community participation work with other Makishi Theatre young colleagues of ours, I was keen to broaden the input of the theatre arts into an active collaborative engagement with NGOs and development practitioners. This would help both the artists and development workers in strengthening their work and enabling community members to strengthen their participation in the development process.

At one time, we linked up with Ann Frommlet, spouse of Wolfram Frommlet, a representative of the Friedrich Naumann Foundation. Ann was keen on helping development - support communications and media in Zambia. She was a nurse, helping the Zambian Helpers Society in their health outreach programmes to areas surrounding Lusaka city.[2] Anne Frommlet brought along Susanna (as Susie was then known) Smith when we went to Kabile, in Lusaka West, where we had some performances in the community. While dealing with the issues of basic health, Susanna was keen on strengthening the voice of community members in the development process.

---

1   This was written in December 2006.
2   The Zambian Helpers Society was founded by Archbishop Emmanuel Milingo, who in 2006 was at cross-purpose with Vatican authorities in Rome over priestly celibacy and marriage issues.

Oxfam's programmes and partners in the 1980s

It was through Susanna Smith, that in the early 1980s I got onto the difficult Mulobezi train to go to Sichili, in Sesheke district, to work with Charles Mwayanguba and fellow health workers on community participation in the primary health care process. And it was in Sichili where Susanna had met Sue Cavanna (see chapter 19), a lifelong spiritual sister of hers, who was a nurse working on primary health care through the Sichili Water Wells and Preventive Health project.

When we were in Ndola and Kitwe, working with the nutrition groups there, Susanna got one of her trophies. Different from the OBE she was later awarded, but I should think the clay pots the women 'marketeers', (as market place traders are called in Zambia), gave her were very precious to her.

Through Susanna, in Oxfam, I as an independent observer, found some warmth in the process and interaction with others in the development process. In Oxfam, I thought, some Quaker roots of peace and goodwill were in evidence.

I began to interact with Oxfam more and more. Those days, in the development process, they called us 'Resource Persons', which, although not very accurate, was a somewhat warmer and more appropriate label than the 'consultant' tag that increased in the late 1990s with corporate direction of the development process.

In addition to my work using theatre and local arts for communication, I sometimes ran separate workshops on community participation. I also got involved in research for the purpose of greater understanding of issues so that there can be more relevant action in the development process. I helped to run workshops for Oxfam partners, staff members and community members of NGOs and CBOs. At one time, I stood in for Oxfam staff on leave. I worked on some reports, including *Adjusting to Adjustment*, published by Oxfam Publications.[3]

Over the decades, in the various issues I helped Oxfam colleagues with, it was a process of great learning and growth, exposing me to many areas of Zambia and the region and the various colleagues I came across. Susanna and colleagues that followed her, using their lodging or office location at 250 Zambezi Road, supported this process.

---

3   Gabriel C. Banda, *Adjusting to Adjustment. Women's and Young People's Responses in a Changing Economy*. Report for Oxfam, Lusaka, June 1990.

The early 1980s provided much challenge and hope for Zambia and the region. Zimbabwe had just become independent in 1980 and the struggle was intensifying in South African-occupied Namibia and in apartheid South Africa itself. Various efforts and support from people of goodwill all over the world were channelled through Zambia.

It was also the time of the worldwide Primary Health Care programme, a participatory holistic approach for sustainable development, launched at Alma Ata in 1980. It made many gains but was later undermined through a coup by the commercialisation process that brought about 'health reforms' directed by the IMF and World Bank, leading to increased deaths and a decline in post-independence gains.

Oxfam was then aiming to work with 'the poorest of the poor' and in remote, isolated areas. They reached out to colleagues and community members in various parts of Zambia. These were CBOs and community projects, and, I believe the experience of direct contact provided valuable insights into people's struggles and joys.

The 1980s were a time for exploring ways in which community members would be more involved in NGOs and development agencies. Tom Scott, VSO Field Director in Zambia, who had initiated an approach which addressed race and personal attitudes in development relationships, also helped. Mike Edwards was interested in the management issue and put in place a modified version that created platforms where partners shared not only their experiences but the direction of Oxfam's approaches. Later, the networking process of partners led to the formation of the local NGO, Unikila.

Oxfam also collaborated with VSO in exploring the use of community animation to increase participation and empowerment of community members in managing the development process. VSO was implementing this approach, and my brother Theo Samuheha was involved in it. The idea was also to get Zambian counterparts to eventually staff projects where VSO expatriates were working. In North-Western Province, besides the experiences at Chiwoma, Kashinakaji, and Kayombo, Oxfam and VSO supported community animation involving refugees in Maheba settlement, near Solwezi town. My visits with Oxfam and VSO staff, and other colleagues at Development Support Forum, helped me to understand many aspects of development challenges in the North-West.

Around 1986, Oxfam supported a team that included Gladys Nakatiwa Mulikita, Peter Yumbe Ntenga, Tapiwa Muchenje, my brother Theo Samuheha, and me, to attend a regional animation course in Zimbabwe. Harare, shortly after Zimbabwe's independence, was a centre for development workshops and conferences. This also helped increase networking amongst activists in the region. On many occasions we compared notes in Harare and Lusaka, and sometimes in Nairobi. Later, in the 1990s, the regional workshop centre moved to Johannesburg and Pretoria.

There were others interested in animation, including Francophone BAM in Luwingu and the Copperbelt, and CUSO. When CUSO phased out of Zambia, they left the women's programme with a heavy popular methodology focus that was to become what we now know as Women for Change. The North-Western Animation Programme NGO, arising from the earlier Oxfam-VSO animation work, with former animators like Alex Kwandu involved, provided hope, although sadly they later disbanded.

In the 1980s, Oxfam supported organisations working on various issues. The support was multi-sectoral, enabling partners to be enriched, and potentially more effective, by the interaction. Through the constant contacts we had in the Oxfam circles, we developed lifelong friendship with persons like Mackenzie Mbewe, a disability activist, his colleagues, and persons working with NGOs and organisations supporting various aspects of the development process.

Through interaction with Oxfam and 250 Zambezi Road, I developed relationships, many still there now, with people in communities, projects, and development organisations. In many towns, there are friends I now meet. I met Catholic priests, our brothers Joe Komakoma and Fr. Afwenya, at Workers' Pastoral Centre, Kitwe, publishing the critical *Workers Challenge* magazine dealing with workers' concerns and development issues on the Copperbelt and nationally.[4]

Those were the times when participation, equity and justice, not only in the society in general but also in groups and institutions, were being strongly

---

4   Note by Robin Palmer: I was sitting in my office in Oxford, reading a copy of the *Workers' Challenge*, which I always enjoyed and admired, when David Bryer, Oxfam's Overseas (International) Director came in. 'Take a look at this,' I said, 'it's great.' He took a look, but was very worried. 'It looks very political,' he said. This must have been the time, c.1990, when the Charity Commissioners were breathing heavily down Oxfam's neck.

promoted. Development action is a coming together of people in various situations to meet challenges. It involves relationships that are beyond office employment. Personal action and development of relationships of friendship and common purpose cannot be divorced from development action. In fact, the collaboration is a requirement of sustainable action and actual meaning and purpose.

Thus we find that in places like Sichili and Senanga; Katete and Kazimule near Chipata town; Malole with their Catholic run Chinchi Wa Bili project; Mumbwa with the Nutrition group and Muyangwe Nursery; and in Maheba in Solwezi; and Chiwoma, Kashinakaji, and Kayompo in Mwinilunga; and Kabompo, Katuta and Chungu in Luwingu; and Kapisha and other areas of the Copperbelt, many people still mention Susanna Smith, Mike Edwards, Pushpanath and Lucy Muyoyeta.

Oxfam's Representatives

I would go to 250 Zambezi Road just to meet the representatives as friends and for discussions on general issues. Of course, it is difficult not to discuss development issues.

In the field and in the office, towering, Susanna was kind, considerate and tolerant, always listening, and bringing out other viewpoints as she helped people to explore their own views. She took a personal interest in the thoughts and situation of others. She had humour and would even laugh at her own experiences. Tolerant of other people's cultures and spiritual beliefs, Susanna was foremost human, rather than a national of Britain. She was a child and citizen of humanity. Susanna was a facilitator, while not imposing herself, creating networks at personal and organisational levels.

Susanna liked Bobby, the fairly friendly white and black dog she kept at Zambezi Road. Perhaps it reminded her of Zambezi Road and Bobby, but even later, at her house in Oxford, she had another alert and supportive dog, similarly painted by nature.

Even after leaving Lusaka, Susanna's association with 250 Zambezi and Zambia continued. Through her book on the Frontline States and the controversial Oxfam campaign on sanctions against apartheid South Africa, she contributed greatly to knowledge and to the campaign.

Our brother Mike Edwards took over habitation of 250 Zambezi Road in 1984. Mike was very analytical and had great capacity for intensive reading and report writing. The annual reports were packed. One time, we sat with Mike, playing drums in his house. Mike and his Brazilian partner Cora were interested in oriental philosophy.

Our brother Pushpanath (1998) approached things with great passion, always placing himself in the situation of project and community members and sometimes, seated cross legged on a chair, exploring with them and challenging with questions of the why's, how's, and the potential way forward.

My sister Lucy Muyoyeta (1993), having had a lot of earlier contact with many projects, communities, and organisations through her extensive and intensive travels and workshops while at SNV and Oxfam, and her passionate concern for justice and the common good, was greatly respected by community members and others in civil society.

Without being controllers, Oxfam helped create and strengthen networks. They helped set up platforms for people from various sectors to be linked. Oxfam helped strengthen skills and capacities. Oxfam was a leader, one organisation others emulated in terms of analysis and human relationships within organisations.

250 Zambezi Road

Around April 1991, when I came back from a tour of the UK, where I shared with Oxfam supporters some challenges of development, I found that the Oxfam office had moved from CUSA House to 250 Zambezi Road, a centre of inspiration. The space and atmosphere contributed greatly to the expanded interaction of Oxfam with partners and of partners amongst themselves. The 250 Zambezi Road premises were the enabling workshop through which the minds of Oxfam Representatives and teams worked.

Oxfam offices and residences, both at CUSA House and 250 Zambezi Road, were hives of activity. Oxfam partners coming in for something else from communities outside Lusaka would just drop in to say hullo to Oxfam staff. Finance and administrative staff would know the faces behind the project files. Oxfam offices and residences were open areas where partners met not only Oxfam staff, but would also arrange to meet fellow partners. 'We will meet at Oxfam.' It offered an open space for interaction and growth of relationships as people acted together from various angles. 250 Zambezi Road, Roma, was then an oasis, a place for nourishment and inspiration.

250 Zambezi Road - A Friend's View

Reaching out with openness, Oxfam collaborated with many organisations and agencies in the 1990s. Together with KEPA, umbrella of Finnish NGOs, and Zambia's Department of Community Development, Oxfam helped support Chipata's women's area associations, whose groups they had worked with since the 1980s, to transform into a district association.

People came to Oxfam from various sectors. One remembers how, in the early 1990s, police vehicles came into 250 Zambezi Road. They arrived with people who had come to pay a courtesy call or to help bring some items from outside Lusaka, where the police officers were members of a disaster preparedness committee or drought action group. This was when the challenges posed by drought had seriously affected Zambia and Oxfam was the lead NGO in the Eastern Province.

And in that drought of the early 1990s, I thought it might be useful to work with Oxfam partners to report the drought situation over a period. Pushpanath and Lucy were in agreement with the process. By long telegrams, we got Oxfam partners in the rural areas to cover many aspects of the situation. These were compiled into editions of a *Drought File*, which UNICEF, government, and others responding to drought used. We spread the network.

Within Zambia, for many, the Oxfam work relationship became a yardstick, an ideal to aim at. They seemed, at least to observers – though things internally may have been different – to have an open and friendly working relationship involving people in Lusaka and Oxford offices. In those days, it was common for correspondence of partners and project implementers to bear 'cc Anne Lloyd Williams', and other persons in Oxford. They seemed to work very well together, Oxford and the Lusaka field office.

When Robin Palmer, Oxford based, came to Lusaka and visited 250 Zambezi Road, he seemed very close to Wilson Kaonza, then doing driving and motor logistic roles. The relationship continued after Wilson retired from Oxfam. On hearing Robin had come to Lusaka, Wilson would drop whatever he was doing and rush to meet Robin. 'Oh, Madala!' Wilson said out of respect for Robin. Details of what they sat or stood discussing for long periods by themselves, only Robin and Wilson can relate. Years ago, Francis Banda, ever inquisitive, asked 'I wonder what those two sit down and talk about for such a long time.'[5]

The Post

It was through Pushpanath that I came into contact with Mike Hall, who was a correspondent with the BBC. One time, Mike brought a colleague of his, Fred M'membe, with whom he was working to start The Post newspaper. My view was that they had to be careful that the monied investors did not control the paper's content and focus. Fred M'membe said he would ensure that they did not. When The Post started in July 1991, I was one of its independent contributors and have kept on writing a column up to the present. [6]

Oxfam was involved in supporting an experiment on rural reporting. Encouraging and working with The Post, some Oxfam partners based in rural areas learnt reporting basics. They sent stories to The Post, giving the paper a rural perspective and voices from the rural areas. I do not know what changed that rural programme. The relationship with The Post continued for long. I do not know the details but I think the Land Cruiser left by Mike was later sold to The Post.

Guy Scott and party cards

It was in 1991 in one of the rooms at 250 Zambezi Road, that Guy Scott visited me. He was interested in my doing a report of rural issues and the challenges Zambia then faced. I said I would be glad to do it as a non-partisan report, something that could be used by anyone trying to deal with the issues. I think our contact declined and phased out when I refused to get an MMD (Movement for Multi-Party Democracy) party card as suggested by Guy, 'just for convenience,' as, 'we are not even a party, we are just a movement.'

I was already critical of some of the disharmony and insincerity in the MMD, something that Guy Scott also noted, moreover was that I had a principle of being non-partisan and would never buy a political party card.

---

5 Note by Robin Palmer: In chapter 10 Lucy Muyoyeta provides part of the answer to the question which puzzled Francis when she wrote about Wilson: 'Amongst his talents included great story telling, farming, and outspokenness. But what I remember most about him is the fact that here was a simple man from a very simple background who never stepped foot in school, but yet was able to hold his own as he took the many Oxfam visitors around the country.' A remarkable man indeed!

6 http://www.postzambia.com

250 Zambezi Road - A Friend's View

Later, Guy Scott was Minister of Agriculture in Frederick Chiluba's November 1991 MMD government.

Oxfam staff

With an intensified IMF and World Bank economic programme, the 1990s were a time of intense onslaught on people's access to basic needs. Development organisations were challenged, with some of their advances swept away. Oxford campaigns people interacted more with Zambezi Road staff and Oxfam partners.

On reflection, perhaps except for one or two, over the life of the Oxfam office's physical presence in Zambia, I found various staff in programmes, administration, and accounts, even ones that have had short stays, very friendly and helpful.

Many programme staff have been essentially activists. My sister Chilufya Kasutu was personally concerned about the direction of issues in the nation and responses of the development fraternity. Then there was sister Lizzie Peme, one of the hardest working persons in the world, very outstanding, committed, analytical and calmly and cheerfully working long beyond office hours. And there was our cheerful and friendly Cynthia Mwase Kasanda, daughter of a theatre colleague Dorcas Habeenzu. Nawina Hamaundu, while learning the works, had kindness in her. There was Simon Tunkanya with his dreads or Rasta hair style. It was also good to meet fellow resource persons, who later established the Institute for Policy Studies, Zambia, which I was at some point closely involved with.

The administrators and accounts persons were keen on the issues. Dorothy Chikula knew many Oxfam partners. Victor Pelekamoyo, ever sharp, brilliant, and seeking relevance, one time went with us to community groups to help them develop basic accounting procedures. Victor had come with Timothy Mbewe, who was in programmes, from Village Industry Service. Our sister Patricia Talale, calm, brilliant, efficient at accounts was concerned about social and spiritual forces.

Malitino Daka later broadened his responsibilities to include managing the Resource Centre. The Resource Centre drew in many partners and those interested in getting information on various aspects of development. In a time when, due to foreign exchange constraints, it was difficult for many people in Zambia to get reading materials from outside, 250 Zambezi Road sent out

Oxfam book tokens. The excellent Oxfam *Field Director's Handbook* (1985) and David Werner's *Where there is No Doctor* masterpiece (1992)[7] were acquired by many people in Zambia through the token scheme.

250 Zambezi Road has even exported staff to Oxfam Headquarters in Oxford: Victor Pelekamoyo and Ernest Williams from accounts and Martin Kalungu-Banda from programmes. Pushpanath is now doing fair trade work, while our dear sister Susie Smith, who found 250 Zambezi Road, was Deputy International Director at the time of her passing away on 23 June 2006.

While the development process involves working together in relationships, friendship is nourished and not forced. Some encounters continue for life. Sichili's Sue Cavanna, an internationalist and universal personality who later for convenience located to Oxford as a base to spring from with her various worldwide networking activities, now uses the cover of a British citizen. Sue was to be a true sister to Susie Smith, supporting her right up to her death from cancer in June 2006. Just a few months earlier, in January 2006, we had a brilliant time of reflection and teamship in Oxford with Sue, Susie, Liz Welsh and Tessa, Sue's talented daughter, who now sings and records her beautiful, expressive music some fifteen years after I held her as a few months old baby.

The challenges of development

The development process requires working together, playing various roles in the team of life. We seek harmony and balance with and within individuals, groups, societies and life itself. It is a part of action towards integrity of life. Relationships continue across land, oceans, and time. In fact, we are remembering through this recollection because many relations do not end; they continue to be part of our lives. Memories rekindle us and let us know what was achieved, what is possible, and what challenges we face.

Various challenges remain. We are now early into the new millennium. Things have changed, some gladness and some sadness. Many people, staff, partners, and community members and their family members we met through Oxfam and 250 Zambezi Road have passed on. Of the animation course team from Zambia, only Gladys Nakatiwa and I remain in 2008. But the method spread to many.

---

7   Now available electronically at *http://www.usadojo.com/articles/where-no-doctor.htm*

Oxfam withdrew from the Eastern Province but, even in 2006 Chipata District Women's Association (DWA), is an example of excellence.

Poverty is higher now, with most men, women, and young people lacking adequate access to basics. Local capacity in various sectors has declined. And HIV and AIDS has become not only a field subject, but an internal challenge to development organisations, whose staff and members have also been victims and affected.

Now, Mike Edwards keeps on writing, in journals and articles, questioning the relevance of development studies. Many years later, into the new millennium, I hope he has made strides in finding parts of the answers.

Life is a cooperative effort involving various parts working together. Realising our strength and strides in the past, in the lives of others and ourselves, we are able to advance in the present. Through those of us who still live and the work of the departed, these departed who contributed to our present lives and whose shared tasks we now carry in this relay of life, we can make great advance.

250 Zambezi Road in Lusaka was a platform and inspiration for networking and action.

A House in Zambia

Gabriel Banda at Sichili, 1982

19. A RECOLLECTION OF 250 ZAMBEZI ROAD IN 1982-83

Sue Cavanna

I arrived back in Zambia in 1982 to do a second two-year stint as a VSO volunteer in Sichili in the Western Province. Charles Mwayanguba and I had set up the Sichili Water Wells Project in 1980 and I was returning to help it get onto a more solid basis.

The nuns in Sichili, who considered water and sanitation as rather 'non-serious' health care, told me in no uncertain terms that there was no point my coming back to Sichili if I did not at once get a vehicle from Oxfam for the water well work. I was told *'come back with a Land Rover or pack your bags'*.

So I returned on the long arduous journey I had just arrived on. A friendly Irish priest gave me a lift to Mulobezi, where I caught the Mulobezi train with its wooden slatted benches to Livingstone, and again by train on to Lusaka. First stop the Oxfam office. I was after that Land Rover.

Susie Smith invited me to stay with her for a few days so that we could talk it over, which we did. In the evenings, I explained the water situation in the Sichili area, and I suspect was rather passionate. After a few evenings' discussion, Susie agreed that we could have a Land Rover for the work. Phew! The Sichili project was back on its feet again and my bags could remain unpacked.

This started a long friendship with Susie Smith and a friendly welcome from her team, Dorothy, Wilson and Daka. It was also the start of a long collaboration with Gabriel Banda.

On occasional visits to Lusaka, hard won breaks that took a lot of negotiation with the Sichili nuns, I stayed with Susie in her house on Jack and Ray Simons' compound. My eyes were opened, a young lass from the remote Lozi bush jettisoned into 250 Zambezi Road, so many comings and goings, so much high level ANC manoeuvring, Umkhonto we Sizwe concerts, walks around Roma in the evenings with Susie, Jack and Ray, amblings around the compound admiring Ray's fruit trees, and endless discussions on Southern Africa – a far cry from helping villages to build their own wells, teaching Charles Mwayanguba to drive, and living in the Catholic mission at Sichili!

A House in Zambia

Sue Cavanna, Sichili, 1982

Sichili Water Wells with Oxfam-gifted Land Rover, 1982

PART SIX:

TWO POSTSCRIPTS, 2004-05

20. SUSANNA 'SUSIE' SMITH RETURNS TO ZAMBIA AFTER SEVENTEEN YEARS, OCTOBER 2004

Gabriel C Banda

Keeping in touch

It was some great homecoming. Twice in this new millennium, Susanna Smith came to Zambia. Then based in Oxford, operating at a wide, worldwide Oxfam level, the issues and events in Zambia would be something she would try to understand and link with common issues and events elsewhere. Together, lessons would be learnt and shared, a common body of knowledge and experience helping all.

After she left Lusaka for Oxfam House in Oxford in 1984, I had kept in touch with Susanna, who in 1981 had been my first contact with Oxfam. Working independently and interacting with staff, partners, and communities, I became a 'friend of Oxfam' in a relationship spanning many succeeding Oxfam field administrations.

I had kept in touch with Susanna, I writing some letters and notes and sending greetings through staff and visitors coming from Oxfam House, Oxford. And on many Christmas times, I would receive a card, many times through Oxfam Zambia's office.

Times I have been in England and Ireland for long and short stays, I had been in touch with Susanna and following her contribution to society. Sometimes when I have been in England, I have stayed at her place.

Even after leaving in 1984, Susanna had maintained contact with Zambia. Besides other processes involving community action, her two books on Namibia and the Frontline States and the impact of apartheid South Africa on them required that she continued the link with Zambia, a nerve centre of the Southern Africa liberation struggle.

A House in Zambia

Susanna Smith returns to Lusaka, October 2004 [1]

During the times she came back to visit in Lusaka, again her presence brought together a building of bridges and links amongst those she had known while in Zambia and while in Oxford and other places. People rekindled their associations and new ones were established. In the new millennium, receptions for her at Ric Goodman's place and Suwilanji Gardens led to links and strengthened relationships. Many of us resolved to strengthen our own paths.

We also had a good reunion with Mrs Dorothy Chikula at Dorothy's place in Roma. In the garden, we reflected on various events, both personal and related to the social development and activism environment.

In work and private life, empathetic to the situation of her colleagues, Susanna would attentively listen to her colleagues' experiences and situations. She did not only consider a person's work situation, but also their personal situation. In discussing ideas, she would participate in making a person think through their situation, thinking with the person but without her dictating the way. She allowed the person to consider various aspects and chart their own directions. She would often be a mover though in the background, working with others and not standing out to market herself as the mover of events.

Now, in October 2004, Susanna Smith was back in Lusaka on a mission. She was concerned about action on HIV and AIDS. What could be done to take action on HIV and AIDS to higher and more effective levels. She saw that leadership was important. Strengthened leadership was needed to mentor various actors and activities involving HIV and AIDS. Leadership involved all fields. Amongst others, Susanna thought of Kenneth Kaunda, Zambia's first president. It was not only that Kenneth Kaunda had come out in the open to talk about the December 1986 HIV-related death of his son Masuzyo. It was not only that Kenneth Kaunda, after leaving state office and active politics, had a foundation focused on dealing with HIV and AIDS. Those were only parts of his reservoir. In Dr Kenneth Kaunda,

---

[1] This visit, her first for seventeen years, marked the genesis of this book. As Susie writes in chapter 6, 'I was surprised and delighted that quite a few of the Oxfam staff there were interested to know more about the history of our Zambezi Road compound in particular, and Oxfam's history in Zambia in general. So, as promised, this is my personal account of a period in the life of this compound in eastern Lusaka, from 1980 to 1984.'

because of his experience in Zambia's struggle for independence and support for the liberation struggle against racism and apartheid in Southern Africa, Susanna Smith felt we could learn something about leadership processes. Sharing his experiences and letting others consider various issues related to his leadership could help with lessons for moving to higher stages the tackling of HIV and AIDS.

The meeting with Kenneth Kaunda, May 2005

So when she returned in May 2005, I was asked to arrange a meeting with Kenneth Kaunda, 'KK', with whom I have been working as a voluntary Special Assistant/Advisor. The meeting took place at KK's residence along Brentwood Drive. That May weekend was bright. Accompanying Susanna were Martin Kalungu-Banda and Ric Goodman, then Oxfam GB's programme manager in Zambia.

The meeting in KK's office and study was warm. Susanna, as usual, was respectful but very relaxed, humorous, joyful, and upbeat. She reminded KK about an incident involving her mother Prudence. It was before Zambia's independence. Prudence, on assignment with the BBC, was to meet Kenneth Kaunda. Due to some detour, KK had arrived late. He had been very polite and kept on apologising for the delay in the interview.

Susanna mentioned some experiences when she was Oxfam Field Director in Zambia. Part of it dealt with experiences with government officials. It was humorous to all. She talked about her own situation, her concern about HIV and AIDS. Susanna talked about KK's role in moving things in Zambia and Africa. There were many things we could learn from that. She began to ask him about some events.

The meeting was more of an open discussion than formal and close-ended. Even the agenda was dynamic. In the discussion, the HIV and AIDS situation was discussed. Issues of leadership were explored. Yet it was remarkable that Susanna had not come with a rigid outline of what she was hoping to achieve. Nor was she rigid about what was to be discussed. Susanna let things evolve. It was a true exploration and sharing together.

She had a longing for something to grow out of the meeting and happen for HIV and AIDS. Yet she had not determined the direction and path. She let it evolve from the discussion. She brought out issues, politely and calmly bringing in some practicality and urgency to the process. And indeed evolve the process did. It was agreed that KK would share his experiences in dealing with various situations. These may not have been directly HIV and AIDS activities. But he was sharing his leadership experiences in many situations. Others were to later sit down with him and explore the experiences. Then quickly Susanna went through the understanding of that outcome again. And it was a shared understanding with KK. The Oxfam Lusaka office and KK's office were to link up and take up the process.

I think the meeting went well and held great potential. Here was something practical that could help in mentoring. As usual, although things were creative and emerging, at the same time there was some method in Susanna's approach. Things not thought of would come out of discussions and sessions. But still, there was process and method in her work.

It would be wrong to say that what she worked on was not clearly thought through, but that she managed to deeply move things without emphasizing and imprisoning the process to fixed outcomes and procedures. She invoked creativity and flowed with what was evolving. The May 2005 meeting with KK again testified to Susanna's great depth of interaction. In many situations, she would be herself, sincere, comfortable with herself while respecting and valuing others she was interacting with.

She would be at peace and at one with men, women, and the young in rural Sichili and Namushakende in Western Zambia, and in Kitwe and Ndola when we went to interact with their district nutrition groups and even had a theatre performance attended by many hundreds of persons and Susanna was honoured with a clay pot. It was an honour from the people. Susanna was at home in development meetings in Lusaka. These experiences she pulled together when she met persons in various situations.

That May 2005 afternoon, in the car park, KK saw Susanna's team off, personally helping with signals for Ric's manoeuvre of the Oxfam vehicle out of the car park. Later, I mentioned to KK about Susanna's cancer treatment, that she was on some medication that required her to get back to Oxford by a certain time, for more treatment. KK commended her strength, courage, and insight.

Meeting Susanna in Oxford, January 2006

The last time I stayed with her in Summertown, Oxford, was January 2006. She was still on cancer treatment. She had months earlier passed a very hard patch but was stronger. She acknowledged that, as many people said, she was better than she had been a few months earlier. The new treatment had worked well with her. She was strong and insisted, when I wanted to help her or do my part by myself, on preparing the food we were eating.

During my stay, I asked for her views on what Kenneth Kaunda might include in his memoirs. Susanna, from what she said she had learnt from the writing experience of her mother Prudence and her own writing, talked about writing as a therapeutic and healing process. She systematically considered KK's phases in public life and suggested approaches in handling the experience. It was a very useful contribution and I later passed it on to KK.

Susanna's funeral and aftermath

On 2 July 2006, I was on a British Airways Lusaka to London flight. I was going to Oxford for Susanna's funeral. She had passed away on 23 June 2006, in Oxford. At Heathrow Airport, I showed the polite immigration officer a photo of Susanna. 'This is Susanna Smith,' I said this to him not to prove my reason of visit, for he had allowed me in already, but to let him know about the greatness of Susanna. He actually took time to look at Susanna on the photo.

The Oxford funeral service was again a time Susanna, this time in death, has acted as a bridge linking many in working together, in many places, for the common good.

After Susanna's transition, Oxfam have made efforts, with others, to involve persons in leadership positions in mentoring and leadership involving HIV and AIDS. In one project, KK was involved. I am sure Susanna's personal approach, learning and sharing without imposing, while allowing others to find their strong ways forward, having smooth relations whose procedure and processes do not overburden the aim of the activity itself, and without her taking personal credit for outcome of processes, can be useful lessons for those involved in finding leadership and mentoring to help action on HIV and AIDS.

As Susanna Smith would have said, I am sure that for many of us involved in this recollection of the 250 Zambezi Road Oxfam office, it has been some healing reflection, following our individual journeys, how we have interacted with others in this relay of life, and how we, acting with others in various places and times, have come to where we are today.

A House in Zambia

Oxfam meets KK, May 2005: Gabriel Banda, Susie Smith, Kenneth Kaunda, Ric Goodman, Martin Kalungu-Banda

21. SUSIE SMITH'S FINAL VISIT TO ZAMBIA, MAY 2005

Martin Kalungu-Banda

A first encounter with Susie

In April 2005, just before my first anniversary of working for Oxfam GB in Oxford, I received a 2004 visit report on Zambia written by Susie Smith via e-mail. I read it, made up my mind and filed it. I had not met Susie in person at the time.

A few days after I had read the Zambia report, I saw a tall lady walk to my desk dressed in bright pink colours. She confidently said, 'You must be Martin.' I nodded in confirmation. She then asked, 'Have you read my report on Zambia?' I answered that I had. I realised then that she was Susie Smith. She asked me why I had not responded to her. I said, 'Do you really want to know what I think about your report?' Sensing my anger, she requested that we go into one of the meeting rooms in order for her to hear my thoughts.

I began to explain to Susie, 'When I read your report, I was very upset with you. I am still very upset. You described my country as if it was one that was about to be rubbed off the world map by HIV.' Susie was looking into my eyes and showing that she was deeply listening. She then said, 'I am very sorry if my report made you feel that way.' She paused for a moment, then continued with a question, 'Martin, how would you describe the HIV and AIDS situation in your country?' Silence. 'Aah...aah', I tried to think on my feet. I went silent. Susie waited patiently.

'Aah...aah', I tried to formulate an answer again. I could not. Suddenly, in an angry voice, I said, 'Of course things are bad, but you have no right to write about other peoples' country in the manner you did. That should have come from us, the nationals of Zambia.'

Gently, Susie asked, 'Martin, are you saying that the problem is not with the way I described the HIV and AIDS situation in Zambia, but that the problem should have been articulated by a Zambian?' At that point I realised that my argument was flawed. I decided to be candid, 'Susie, it hurts to think about one's country in the words you have used. I was upset with you because I did not want the description you gave of my country to be true. I have lost many relatives to AIDS. Each time I visit home, the first thing every household I go to gives me is a litany of those who have passed away while I was out of the country. Mind you, I am in Zambia nearly every three months.'

Susie moved from her seat and sat next to me. Placing her right hand on my shoulder, she said, 'Martin, I cannot pretend that I fully understand what you and your people are going through. However, I lived in Zambia long enough to have an appreciation of how you feel. I truly share in your pain. I equally share your fears.'

Susie and I continued our conversation. In the end we reached two agreements. First, we agreed on the hypothesis that part of what compounded the HIV and AIDS situation in Zambia could be a deep-seated denial of the existence and gravity of the pandemic. Second, we agreed that we test our hypothesis with Oxfam GB staff in the following countries: Zambia, Mozambique and Angola. Susie challenged me to develop a process through which we could engage in genuine conversations with our staff in the three countries. Although I am not a specialist on HIV and AIDS, I took up the challenge. I fell back on the learning I had picked from Lance Secretan's leadership programmes and drafted a three and a half day process.

Conversations about AIDS with Oxfam staff

In Zambia, the conversation in May 2005 started with focusing our staff on the notion that they were leaders in their own right who had both the right and the responsibility to attend to problems confronting their society. On the second day, we went and engaged in dialogue with 'fellow' leaders in government, church, business, and civil society. Upon learning from others, we came together to share what we had heard. Towards the end of the day, Susie and I asked the participants, 'To what extent are you personally impacted by HIV?' The responses were cautious and measured, 'I have heard of some distant friends who have been affected by the pandemic' or 'I have come across the problem in our development work.'

On the third day, we used techniques to help participants practise how to confront problems affecting them. We then asked the same question, 'To what extent are you personally impacted by HIV?' The answers somewhat changed to 'I have lost distant relatives to the pandemic.' On the fourth day, after 'crowning' ourselves with the title of being change agents, we posed the same question, 'To what extent are you personally impacted by HIV?'

The following answers were given, 'I have lost brothers and sisters to AIDS', or 'I am looking after a number of orphans left by my siblings,' or 'I am nursing my own brother affected by AIDS in my home.' Other answers were, 'I could not talk about how affected I was by HIV because everybody came to work behaving as if they only came across the problem through the work we do as an organisation'; 'I have never undergone an HIV test because I am terrified of the implications of the results.'

What does the President think about AIDS?

On the fifth day of our stay in Lusaka, as we were having breakfast, Susie asked, 'What do you think are the President's thoughts and feelings about the HIV situation in Zambia?' Not knowing where she was leading to, I said, 'I do not know'. 'It would be great to know,' she went on. I remained silent. 'Do you think you could find a way of us meeting and asking him this question.' I knew Susie was serious. 'I will make a few phone calls and see whether we can secure an appointment with the President,' I assured her.

In the course of the day I managed to speak to the President. He agreed that we visit him the following day. Just after we shook hands with the President (Levy Mwanawasa), Susie said, 'Mr President, thank you very much for having us in your office. Zambia is like my second home because my career started in earnest from Zambia.' 'Is that so?' The President mused. 'I asked Martin for the opportunity to meet with you because I would like to know what really keeps you awake at night as you lead this country?' There was silence in the room. The President repositioned himself in his seat and cleared his throat.

'There are many problems that keep me awake,' the President began. 'I worry about the poverty of the majority of our people. The growth in the economy is not yet good enough to begin to reverse the poverty that is impacting many people. However, if there is any one issue that worries me, it is the problem of AIDS. I fear that if we do not do something creative and immediate about the situation, it is possible to wake up one day and there are no people to lead.'

'Mr President, what are some of the things that would make you feel that the problem of HIV and AIDS is being addressed?' Susie asked. Again, some silence reigned. 'I would love a situation where just as I have someone among my advisers who brings to my attention on a daily basis economic issues, there is someone who focuses my attention on HIV and AIDS. Budgetary constraints and bureaucracy inhibit the speed with which I would want to do this.'

'That is a noble idea, Mr President,' Susie complimented. 'I am sure if this is the way you would want to go, there are people out there who would find your idea worthy of support.' The President responded that he was surely interested and would appreciate Susie's and Oxfam's help. Susie promised the President to find the resources that would allow him to hire an adviser for HIV and AIDS.

While I was working with her in Zambia, Susie shared with me that she knew she did not have many days to walk the earth. She said, 'Martin, because we are working together, you need to know this. I am dying very soon.' She knew that she had shocked me. She paused for me to take in the shock. 'I have been fighting with cancer for a number of years now. I do not think I have many years to live. I wanted you to know this because in the next few months, we will be working as colleagues and anything could happen to me.' I did not know how to respond. It was the first time I was facing someone who talked about her own possible death as if it was some event to gladly wait for.

A few months later, I was the bearer of the terrible news to the President that Susie had died. After the President expressed his condolences he asked, 'Where does Susie's death leave the discussion I had with her?' I answered, 'Your Excellency, I am pleased to say that Oxfam GB has found some well wishers who would like to support your idea.' 'That's a very good way of honouring the life of one of you. Please, draft for me the terms of reference for the role.'

Inspired by Susie's conversations on HIV and AIDS with the Oxfam Zambia staff, we (Oxfam GB in partnership with the Society for Organisational Learning) continued the conversation by bringing together a cross-sector group of people with the common intention to bring innovation to fighting the pandemic. The group is composed of leaders from business, government, the churches, trade unions, and civil society. It has constituted itself into a trust known as the Trust for Collective Action on HIV & AIDS in Zambia (TCAHZa). It is trying to respond to HIV and AIDS by learning to observe the situation with an open mind, open heart and open will; then take time to retreat in order to make sense of what it has observed;

thereafter quickly move into implementing (prototyping) the new insights emerging in order to pick the intelligence that lies in our hands. It is hoped these lessons will then justify the scaling-up of any such initiative.

Susie is regarded by the trust as the spirit that inspired its work.

In Zambia Susie lives.

Outside State House, May 2005: Susie Smith, Chilufya Kasutu, Ric Goodman, Martin Kalungu-Banda

PART SEVEN:

CLOSING THOUGHTS

22. OBITUARY FOR SUSANNA 'SUSIE' SMITH

Kevin Watkins [1]

Susanna 'Susie' Smith, charity administrator and campaigner, born May 28 1951; died June 23 2006.

Susie Smith, who has died aged fifty five of cancer, was one of the real heroes in the fight against global poverty. The vision, humanity and intellectual honesty she showed during a thirty year career with Oxfam changed the world and touched countless lives. Working first as Field Director in Zambia, then as a researcher and senior manager at head office, she played a key role in transforming Oxfam, rewriting the rules of engagement on poverty, recasting Britain's charity laws and supporting the fight against HIV and Aids.

She was only twenty eight when she was sent to run the agency's programmes in Zambia and Malawi, as Oxfam's youngest ever Field Director. To understand what she achieved, you have to enter a different development universe. Forget Bono, Live Aid, the rich countries' commitments on aid and debt, and cuddly versions of the World Bank and the International Monetary Fund.

Susie arrived in Zambia in 1980, just after Margaret Thatcher moved into Downing Street, and at the start of the dark age in international development. Her new home was a region on the frontline of a brutal war of aggression conducted by apartheid South Africa. She was living in a country in the throes of a devastating debt crisis. The IMF-World Bank was using Zambia as a laboratory for structural adjustment programmes that made monetarism in Britain look like a Keynesian stroll in the park.

Meanwhile, the British Government was slashing aid budgets, ignoring the debt problem and turning a blind eye to the ravages of apartheid - for good measure, 'political campaigning' on development was ruled out-of-bounds by charity laws crafted in the 19th century.

Having gone to Zambia as an enthusiastic believer in the power of projects, Susie was too honest, too intelligent, and too committed to Africa to play a game in which the rules were loaded against the poor. Why write

---

1   This is a slightly revised version of the obituary which appeared in The Guardian on 29 June 2006.

cheques for a few water pumps in remote villages when debt, IMF-World Bank policies, apartheid aggression and the indifference of the rich world were destroying the fabric of local society? The experience transformed her understanding of development. Above all, it persuaded her that charity without social justice was an indulgence, the politics of the empty gesture.

It was during Susie's tenure that the compound at 250 Zambezi Road, Lusaka, where she lived as an Oxfam tenant, gained its legendary status as a radical hub. Owned by prominent ANC activists Jack and Ray Simons – and with Thabo Mbeki a frequent visitor – at one stage it provided a base for the constitutional committee that drew up the precursor to today's South African Constitution.

Born in London, Susie was educated at Dartington Hall School, Devon. It was her mother, Pru Smith, a BBC journalist and South African exile, who sparked her love of Africa. Two years after graduating in philosophy from Newcastle University in 1973, Susie started her career with Oxfam, rising rapidly through the ranks before going to Southern Africa.

After giving birth to her daughter, Sarah, she switched to policy research, returning to Oxford in 1985 to join Oxfam's small, but formidably effective, Public Affairs Unit (PAU). Her first book, *Namibia: a Violation of Trust* (1986), caused a minor storm. In it she documented, in copious detail, how the British Government was soft-pedalling in its opposition to apartheid South Africa's illegal occupation of what was then South-West Africa (now Namibia).

Her second book, *Front Line Africa* (1990), raised the stakes - along with the hackles - of the Charity Commission. Drawing on Oxfam's field experience and rigorous academic research, the book charted the impact of apartheid, debt and unfair trade rules on the lives of ordinary people. Brilliantly researched, well written and passionately argued, it comprehensively demolished the argument that development charities could, and should, keep politics out of development.

Oxfam was hauled before the Charity Commission, found guilty of exceeding its charitable mandate and told to behave itself. But the floodgates had been opened. After a few years of stand-off, the charity law was interpreted more flexibly. I doubt that anybody in NGOs today worries too much about bringing politics into development. They owe a vote of thanks to Susie for that.

After 1992 her career took a new course. Convinced that Oxfam was punching below its weight, she directed her energies towards organisational development. Working first as Executive Assistant to the Director and, from

Obituary for Susanna 'Susie' Smith

1998, as Deputy International Director, she played a critical role in making Oxfam the force it is today. Mercifully unaddicted to management consultancy fads and deeply averse to hierarchy, she achieved change by changing minds, by mentoring people - and by leading from the front.

One of her greatest attributes was her willingness to step outside the comfort zone. She was uncompromising in addressing the international causes of poverty. But she was also brutally honest about the impact of corruption and indifference to the poor on the part of governments in Africa and elsewhere. Never renowned for her diplomatic skills, she told it like it was.

First diagnosed with cancer in 1997, Susie suffered a recurrence three years ago. After that, she worked tirelessly to develop Oxfam's HIV and AIDS programme, especially in Southern Africa. Her courage defied description. Over the past year, as her illness progressed, she was visibly in increasing pain. That did not stop her undertaking gruelling trips to Angola, Mozambique, Malawi and, once again, to Zambia. She believed she was helping others to make a difference - and she was. She was made an OBE in 1999.

Susie was an inspiration. Clever, thoughtful, articulate, passionate and persuasive, she was everything that one could want in a colleague, and more. In a sometimes cynical development world, her humility, gentleness and dogged unwillingness to embrace received wisdom shone like a beacon. But there is so much more that we shall miss: her love of life, her wicked sense of humour, her passion for poetry and gardens, her pink and purple clothes, and her talent for bringing people together. Being a mother was a source of joy and happiness in Susie's life; it was her love for Sarah that gave her the will to fight on so courageously for so long.

In September 2005, a group of friends, family and colleagues gathered with Susie at a farmhouse in Oxford to celebrate her thirty years with Oxfam. We knew - and she knew - that her time was coming to an end. It is a rare privilege to be able to tell someone before they die how much they are loved, cherished and respected. We had that privilege.

There is a Bernard O'Donaghue poem that ends:

Happy the man who, dying can
Place his hand on his heart and say:
'At least I didn't neglect to tell
The thrush how beautifully she sings.'

A House in Zambia

Susie died knowing how beautifully we thought she sang. She had iron in her soul and gold in her heart. She lit up the world and made it a better place.

Her daughter survives her.

Kevin Watkins

Susie's farewell party, September 2005

Obituary for Susanna 'Susie' Smith

Susie – the 'official' Oxfam photo

23. CLOSING THOUGHTS

Izzy Birch (1986-93)

The 'Zammers' – as the Oxfam team in Lusaka were fondly christened by those of us working in Oxfam House [1] – inspired affection and respect in all who met them. Some of them would visit Oxford from time to time, helping to cement the professional ties which had been established (in those pre-Skype days) via the truncated and often cryptic medium of the telex. Requests for long wheel base Land Cruisers for shipment via Beira in Mozambique would be followed in the next line by pleas for tablets or treats for Bobby the dog, to be shipped in the luggage of whichever kind soul could be prevailed upon to take them on their next trip south.

In 1988 I was lucky enough to make that journey. I was in the capital for only a few days and remember little about 250 Zambezi Road. But it was my first visit to Africa, and for that reason alone Lusaka occupies a special place in my affections. I was lucky too in that my first exposure to this rather strange world of 'development' was under the tutelage of staff and partners of the calibre Gabriel Banda describes in chapter 18.

One striking feature of this collection is how several of the authors came into contact with 250 Zambezi Road and its occupants at a similarly formative time in their lives. For Susie Smith, life with Jack and Ray Simons was 'the best entrée I could possibly ever have had' to their world. For Lazarous Chewe, who started work as a young guard at the compound almost a decade later, his relationships with the Simons and with Oxfam gave him the foundations from which to build a very different life for himself. For Mike Edwards, his time there with Oxfam 'was what formed me as a person' while for Lucy Muyoyeta, 'the times at 250 Zambezi Road remain the best of my years professionally and personally, and I have everlasting fond memories.'

At the other end of the spectrum the reader is also struck by the wisdom and humanity of the elderly Jack and Ray Simons – by the impact of their 'critical intelligences', in Hugh Macmillan's phrase, on the young Oxfam

---

1 Izzy Birch was Oxfam's Desk Administrator for the Zambia programme based in Oxford between 1986 and 1993.

representatives who were their tenants, and by the generosity and the respect they showed to all: 'I had a measure of how they valued each and every person no matter how callow,' recalls Anne Lloyd-Williams.

One of the most moving stories in this collection is Lazarous Chewe's account of the elderly Nelson Mandela embracing the elderly Jack Simons after his release from prison. At first, Lazarous was not entirely sure who the elderly visitor was. Several other contributors became aware of the history of the house and the identity of their landlords only over time. 'Slowly, organically, I began to realize who I was living with,' wrote Susie Smith. For Lucy Muyoyeta, it took a while to realize 'just how famous these two were'. In the 1980s Zambia was a focal point for the liberation struggle in Southern Africa, and through the gates of 250 Zambezi Road passed a formidable line-up of the region's political activists. According to Hugh Macmillan, 'there can be few houses... in Lusaka that have welcomed so many interesting people or witnessed so much history in the making.'

For Oxfam too, in its more modest way, the compound was always 'open house'. 250 Zambezi Road was where Oxfam's partner organisations knew that they would find hospitality and the chance to meet with friends and colleagues. 'We used to keep the gate open,' writes Pushpanath, in both a literal and metaphorical sense. For the Simons too, the gate was always open: several authors recall with pleasure accompanying them on their walks around the neighbourhood in the early evening.

The sadness in this collection is its reminder of the many who are no longer with us. Peter Wiles remembers the staff from Oxfam's Southern Africa programme who died before their time. Jack and Ray both died back home in South Africa. Many of the Zammers – including Francis Banda, Nawina Hamaundu, Christine Chinzewe, Michael Kumwenda and members of the Burning Youth band, several representatives from partner organisations and, most recently, Susie herself – have all passed away. But perhaps a little of their spirit lives on in these recollections of a place which was a part of all their lives and which, in all its incarnations, was for so many 'an oasis, a place for nourishment and inspiration'. Gabriel Banda's tribute to the place might equally well apply to the people who made it so.

Closing Thoughts

Sue Cavanna & Izzy Birch, 2000

www.ingramcontent.com/pod-product-compliance
Lightning Source LLC
Chambersburg PA
CBHW021407290426
44108CB00010B/422